FINISH LINE

Reading

for the Common Core State Standards

Continental

Acknowledgments

Illustrations: Page 11, 42, 56, 59, 69, 77, 89, 98, 100, 107, 122, 126, 143, 144, 163, 169: Laurie Conley; Page 28: Chris Vallo; Page 32: Margaret Lindmark; Page 115: Zeke Smith; Page 122: Doris Ettlinger; Page 217: Harry Norcross

Photographs: Page 17: Robert Hooke; Page 45: Sun Guoting; Page 52: Image used under Creative Commons from Brego; Page 86, *above:* Image used under Creative Commons from Jared C. Benedict; *bottom left:* Image used under Creative Commons from CeCILL from Rama; Page 93: Image used under Creative Commons form Dehk; Page 113: Image used under Creative Commons from jeffk; Page 130: Library of Congress, Prints and Photographs Division, LC-USZC4-1298; Page 137: NASA/JPL-Caltech/ASU; Page 148: Library of Congress, Prints and Photographs Division, LC-DIG-cwpb_0356 DLC; Page 151: Map reproduction courtesy of the Norman B. Leventhal Map Center at the Boston Public Library; Page 173: Library of Congress, Prints and Photographs Division, LC-DIG-cwpb_03242; Page 181: Richard Canton Woodville; Page 187: William Simpson; Page 192, *wolf:* U.S. Fish and Wildlife Service; *dog:* Image used under Creative Commons from Smallbones; *skulls:* National Park Service; Page 203: Images used under Creative Commons from Gwillhickers

Page 134: "Testimony" is from *The Poems of Charles Reznikoff: 1918–1975* by Charles Reznikoff, edited by Seamus Cooney. Reprinted by permission of Black Sparrow Books, an imprint of David R. Godine, Publisher, Inc. Copyright ©2005 by Charles Reznikoff, edited by Seamus Cooney

ISBN 978-0-8454-6749-7

Copyright © 2011 The Continental Press, Inc.

Table of Contents

Welcome to Finish Line Reading for the Common Core State Standards

This book will give you practice in the reading and comprehension skills necessary to be an effective reader. It will also help you to prepare for reading tests that assess your skills and knowledge.

The material in this book is aligned to the Common Core State Standards for English Language Arts and Literacy in History, Social Studies, Science, and Technical Subjects. The Common Core State Standards (CCSS) build on the education standards developed by the states. The CCSS "specify what literacy skills and understandings are required for college and career readiness in multiple disciplines." This book will help you practice the skills necessary to be a literate person in the 21st century.

In the lessons of this book, you will read informational and literary selections and then answer multiple-choice and short-response questions about them. The lessons in this book are in three parts:

- The first part introduces the reading skill you are going to study and explains what it is and how you use it.

- The second part is called Guided Practice. You will get more than just practice here; you will get help. You will read a story, poem, or nonfiction article and answer questions about it. After each question, you will find an explanation of the correct answer. So you will answer questions and find out right away if you were correct. You will also learn why one answer is correct and others are not.

- The third part is called Test Yourself. Here you will read a passage and answer the questions on your own.

When you finish each unit, you will complete a Review Lesson to show what you have learned in that unit. This will help you evaluate the progress you are making. After you have finished all of the lessons and units, you will take a Practice Test at the end of the book.

Now you are ready to begin using this book. Good Luck!

Vocabulary Development

You're living in a sea of words. They describe what you perceive with your senses and what you conceive with your thoughts. You use words when you speak, when you listen, and when you read. Even when you're looking at wordless images on a computer or movie screen, what you see is filtered through your brain as words. The more words you know, the better equipped you are to understand and consider new ideas—and to come up with new ideas of your own.

You've been using words and learning new ones ever since you were a baby. You learn some of them by listening, just as you did back then, but now you can learn a lot more of them by reading. This unit is all about vocabulary development—learning the meanings of new words and how to use them as you read.

⬤ **In Lesson 1,** you'll learn about context clues—how to figure out what new words mean by relating to other words in a sentence or paragraph that you already know. You'll learn how to differentiate among the meanings of words that can have more than one meaning. And you'll learn how to add new words to your vocabulary by adding parts to other words.

⬤ **Lesson 2** is about words that don't mean exactly what they say. You'll learn how to recognize and interpret figurative language—words that writers use to guide you in perceiving things in new and imaginative ways, especially in poetry. You'll learn how to recognize words that have acquired meaning in our language from myth, history, and literature. You'll learn how to determine the meaning of words by noting their relationships to other words. And you'll learn how to distinguish among the meanings of words that mean almost the same thing as one another, but that people respond to emotionally in very different ways.

⬤ **Lesson 3** is about those words that you may not use in conversation or encounter regularly in your casual reading, but that are important to know when you're reading about specific topics. You'll learn how to use context clues to discover the meanings of those special terms used in science, social studies, and other subjects.

Word Meanings

L.7.4, RL.7.4, RI.7.4, RH.7.4, RST.7.4

How do you learn new words? There are times when you're reading, or when people are speaking, that you hear a word that's unfamiliar to you. You may ask someone what it means or consult a dictionary or online reference. Often, though, you can figure out its meaning through **context clues**—by noting how the word is used in a sentence or paragraph and how it relates to words that you know and to ideas that you understand.

Context Clues

Read this sentence from Dr. Martin Luther King, Jr.'s famous "I Have a Dream" speech of 1963:

There will be neither rest nor tranquility in America until the Negro is granted his citizenship rights.

Do you know what the word tranquility means? If not, there are clues that let you figure out its meaning from the rest of the sentence. First, you can tell by the way it is used in the sentence that it is a noun. Dr. King uses it in parallel with a noun that you know well: *rest*. You can tell he means that America will be troubled and not at peace with itself as long as racism exists. You can guess that tranquility is a synonym for *rest* and means "peace" or "calm."

Context clues may come in several forms:

Context Clues

Synonyms	Words that have nearly the same meanings
Examples	Words that show what another word means
Definitions	Words that tell what another word means
Descriptions	Words that tell you more about a word, such as by comparison or by explaining an action it causes

Synonyms

Sometimes, as in the sentence on page 6 from Dr. King's speech, a word in the sentence means nearly the same thing as the word you don't know. If you know one word, you can figure out the other.

His avarice had made Billingsley the richest man in town, but he was universally despised for his greed.

The word avarice may be unfamiliar to you, but the second part of the sentence contains a synonym. The context shows you that avarice means "greed."

Examples

In other paragraphs, you can figure out the meaning of an unknown word by examples that point to what it means.

Like the ancient Romans, the Aztecs were a bellicose nation who by 1500 had conquered all of central Mexico.

What does bellicose mean? The context shows that it's an adjective, and the example compares the Aztecs with the ancient Romans. You know something about the Romans and their history. That knowledge and the verb *conquered* lets you figure out that bellicose means "warlike."

Definitions

Sometimes a word is directly defined in context. Look for definitions in these sentences:

"The arachnoid creatures of this planet spin webs to trap their prey, just like spiders on Earth," Klaven warned.

Arachnoid is a word that you probably have not heard before. The context shows you immediately that it's an adjective, describing *creatures*, and the rest of the sentence defines the creatures. You can tell from Klaven's definition that arachnoid means "spiderlike."

Descriptions

Sometimes a sentence will contain a description to tell you what a word means. The description might be a *comparison* with something you know. Or, it might show you a *relationship* between the new word and the one you know.

> The senator's economic plan is nothing but a conjuror's trick, like making a bouquet of flowers appear.

You may not know the word <u>conjuror</u>, but the context tells you that it is someone who performs tricks such as you'd see in a magic act. You can tell from this relationship that a <u>conjuror</u> is "someone who performs magic by illusion."

Guided Practice

Read the passage. Then answer the questions.

Now, the canoe was <u>athwart</u> the river, sideways to the current. Peter dug in with his paddle and shifted his weight to keep the boat from <u>capsizing</u>. "If we do tip over," he yelled, "go over the rapids feet first. Your life jacket is <u>buoyant</u>, so you won't go under. The danger is in hitting your head on a rock." I nodded, still holding the splintered paddle in hope that it might not be as <u>dysfunctional</u> as it looked.

Make sure you know the exact meaning of the new words in this passage by checking their meaning in a print or online dictionary.

The word <u>athwart</u> means _____.

A dangerous

B gliding easily on

C bobbing up and down

D across from side to side

 You can find a synonym of <u>athwart</u> in the same sentence. The context tells you, too, that the word is a preposition, showing the boat's position relative to the river. The boat is not gliding easily or bobbing up and down. The *situation* is dangerous, but the boat is sideways in the river. Choice D is the correct answer.

The word capsizing means ____.

A leaking

B stopping

C tipping over

D reaching land

The word is defined in the next sentence, and the context shows you that Peter is not worried about the boat leaking, stopping, or reaching land. Choice C is the correct answer.

What does buoyant mean?

_____

To understand the word buoyant, consider the context of what Peter is saying. He's talking about the possibility of the boat tipping over and reassuring the narrator that he won't go under. Here is a sample answer:

The word buoyant means "able to float."

What does the word dysfunctional mean? Explain your answer.

_____

_____

You may not know the word dysfunctional, but the context gives you an example of something that the word describes: a broken paddle. Your answer could be something like this:

Dysfunctional means "useless." The word applies to a broken canoe paddle.

Words With Multiple Meanings

The word current in the paragraph on page 8 can have more than one meaning. You probably know many such words. A dictionary will list each meaning separately, usually with a number in front. The different meanings may be spelled and even pronounced alike. But if you don't know all the meanings, you may not understand what you're reading. Here are some of the meanings of the word current:

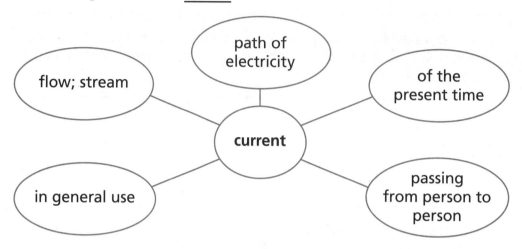

When you come across a word like current in a sentence, use context clues to find out its meaning. Notice how it is used in the sentence. Is it a noun, verb, adjective, or some other part of speech?

> **We have a class discussion of current events every Monday.**

In this sentence, current is clearly an adjective, describing the noun *events*. The context shows you that it means "happening at the present time."

Guided Practice

Tamar raised her binoculars toward the <u>defile</u>. At first she <u>distinguished</u> nothing but the rocks and trees. Then she saw them: a <u>score</u> or more of them, carrying branches before them as camouflage. They were picking their way down the slope and spreading out in a <u>rank</u> when they reached level ground.

The word <u>defile</u> in this passage means _____.

A   to make dirty

B   to walk in single file

C   a steep and narrow valley

D   to cheapen, make unsuitable

As used in the passage, the word <u>defile</u> is plainly a noun. That eliminates choices A, B, and D, which define verbs. The context, too, tells you that the word as used here is a geographical term. The correct answer is choice C.

What does the word <u>distinguished</u> mean in this passage?

   A famous

   B made out plainly

   C separated into groups

   D saw a difference between

> <u>Distinguished</u> in this passage is a verb, so you can eliminate choice A, which defines an adjective. Mentally substitute the other definitions in the sentence. Tamar is not separating anything into groups or noting differences. She's able to plainly see people through her binoculars. Choice B is the correct answer.

What does the word <u>score</u> mean in this passage?

_____

> The word <u>score</u> can have to do with a tally of points in a game or with making a mark on something. However, here it plainly refers to a number, as in Abraham Lincoln's "Fourscore and seven years ago…."

     The word <u>score</u> in the passage means "twenty."

What does the word <u>rank</u> mean in this passage? Explain your answer.

_____

_____

> <u>Rank</u> is a word with many meanings. As an adjective, it can mean "growing thickly" or "bad smelling" (among other things). As a verb, it can mean "to list in order." However, in this passage it's used as a noun. Here is a sample answer:

     <u>Rank</u> means "a row of people side by side." You can tell it's a noun, and it refers to a group spreading out.

UNIT 1
Vocabulary Development

Using Prefixes, Suffixes, and Root Words _____

Often, you can understand new words because they consist of familiar words with new parts added on. A **prefix** is a part of a word added to the beginning of the word that changes the meaning of the word. If you know that media means "means of communication," and you know that the prefix *multi-* means "many," you can figure out that multimedia means "using several forms of communication."

A **suffix** is a part added to the end of a word that changes the meaning of the word. If you know that the word patriot means "one who loves her country," and you know that the suffix *-ic* means "of or relating to," you can figure out that a patriotic song is "one that celebrates love for one's country."

Most prefixes and suffixes come from Latin and Greek words. For example, the prefix *quad-* comes from the Latin word for "four." Knowing that helps you understand the meaning of words like "quadrilateral" and "quadruped."

Some Common Prefixes

Prefix	Meaning	Example
anti-	against	antidote
auto-	self	automatic
co-	together	cohesive
dis-	opposite of, lack of, not	dishonest, disbelieve
extra-	outside; beyond	extraordinary
in-, im-, il-	in, into, or not	injection, incredible
mid-	middle, in the middle of	midnight
mis-	bad or wrong	misrepresent
multi-	many	multipurpose
post-	after	postscript
pre-	before	precooked
semi-	half	semitrailer
tele-	at a distance	telephone
trans-	through, over, across	transaction
uni-	one	universe

Some Common Suffixes

Suffix	Meaning	Example
-able, -ible	able to, or tending to do or be	believ*able*, divis*ible*
-ance, -ence	state, condition, or action	import*ance*, persist*ence*
-en	to cause to be, or made of	weak*en*, wood*en*
-ful	full of, or able to	power*ful*, harm*ful*
-ic	of, or relating to	atmospher*ic*
-ion	act, or condition of	opin*ion*, relat*ion*
-ist	one who is or does something	journal*ist*
-less	without, or cannot be	home*less*, count*less*
-ment	the act of, or result of	embarrass*ment*
-ous	full of, or characterized by	joy*ous*, odor*ous*
-ship	condition, or state of	partner*ship*, owner*ship*
-tion, -ation	the act of	prepar*ation*
-y	like, or tending to be	stick*y*

Prefixes and suffixes may be added to **root words** to make new words. If you know the meaning of a root word, and you know the meaning of a prefix or suffix, you can usually figure out the meaning of new words.

Many common root words come from Greek and Latin words, too. For example, the word bellicose on page 7 comes from the Latin word *bellum*, meaning "war." If you know that the root bell has to do with war, you can easily figure out the meaning of words like bellicose and belligerent, and what a rebel is and does.

Some Common Greek and Latin Roots

Root	Meaning	Example
aqua	water	aquatic
aud	hear	audition
bio	life	biology
chron	time	chronological
cred	believe	discredit
dict	speak	predict
geo	earth (Greek)	geometric
graph	write, draw, print	photograph
ped, pod	foot	quadruped, tripod
phono	sound	headphones
photo	light	photon
scrib, scrip	write	script
terr	earth (Latin)	terrestrial
vert, vers	turn	reversal
vid, vis	see	invisible
voc	speak, voice, call	vocation, vocalist

Guided Practice

Read the passage. Then answer the questions.

Grandison's performance last night gives credence to the idea that he is the finest actor of our time. His multidimensional portrayal of the relatively minor character Barnaby stole the show from the lead performers. He invests with poetic nuance even a seemingly ordinary line like "Please close the door."

The word <u>credence</u> means _____.

   A   honor

   B   power

   C   believability

   D   understanding

   You may not know the word <u>credence</u>, but you know words like *credit* and *incredible,* so you know it has something to do with believing. Substitute each word in the sentence, and you'll see that it has nothing to do with honor, power, or understanding. The correct answer is choice C.

What does the word <u>multidimensional</u> mean?

_____

_____

   You know that the prefix *multi-* means "many," and your knowledge of words like *natural* and *ornamental* tells you that the suffix *-al* means "having the nature of." Here is a sample answer:

   <u>Multidimensional</u> means "having many dimensions," or "being able to play many different kinds of parts."

What does <u>poetic</u> mean?

   A   like a poem

   B   full of poetry

   C   without poetry

   D   able to write a poem

   You know that the suffix *-ic* means "of, or relating to." Think of words like *heroic* and *patriotic,* and you'll recognize that Mr. Granderson speaks his lines *like* a poem, with meaning beyond the literal sense of the words. The correct answer is choice A.

Test Yourself

Robert Hooke (1635–1703)

by Anne Perkins

If they had awarded Nobel prizes in the 17th century, Robert Hooke would have merited half a dozen of them. His accomplishments in physics include the invention of the universal joint, still used today in cars. Medicine? He invented an early prototype of the respirator. Chemistry? He was the first to work out the role of air in combustion. He invented or improved meteorological instruments, collaborated with most of the leading scientists of his day, and demonstrated new experiments to the Royal Society of London, the first organization dedicated to increasing scientific knowledge.

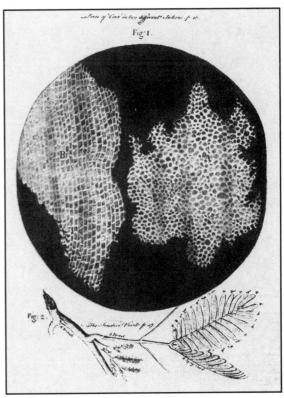

Hooke made his most important contributions in biology. He built one of the first compound microscopes. It was easier to use than the simple microscopes other scientists were using. Looking at plant tissue with this new instrument, Hooke discovered cells, which he named. He published his detailed, beautiful drawings of his microscopic discoveries in a book called *Micrographia.* The book became a bestseller of its time. Hooke also looked at fossils under the microscope and was the first to understand what they were. He realized they meant that species have appeared and gone extinct as long as life has existed on Earth. Other scientists had called fossils "sports of nature," stones and minerals that only looked like living things. Hooke concluded that the shell-like fossils he examined were "the shells of certain shell-fishes, which, either by some deluge, inundation, earthquake, or some such other means, came to be thrown to that place, and there to be filled by some kind of mud or clay…." Because fossil shells were often found inland or high on mountains, Hooke proposed that these places "have been heretofore under the water," and were forced upwards by "the effects of some very great earthquake."

No likeness exists of Hooke. His famous colleague and rival, Isaac Newton, was jealous of his achievements and worked to discredit him after his death. Perhaps these two facts explain why few people today know about the work of this great scientist.

1 The word <u>merited</u> means ____.

   A deserved

   B explained

   C discovered

   D understood

2 <u>Accomplishments</u> means ____.

   A things achieved

   B without achieving

   C able to be achieved

   D the act of achieving

3 A <u>prototype</u> is ____.

   A an improvement

   B an original or model

   C a medical instrument

   D the best thing of its kind

4 The word <u>collaborated</u> means ____.

   A did not work

   B worked together

   C worked many times

   D worked in competition

5 In the second paragraph, what does the word <u>compound</u> mean?

    A to mix or combine

    B to increase or multiply

    C made up of several parts

    D an enclosed group of buildings

6 Explain your answer to question 5.

_____

_____

_____

_____

_____

7 The word <u>cells</u> as used in this passage means _____.

    A small rooms

    B basic units of living matter

    C containers that produce electricity

    D small groups of people within a larger organization

8 The word <u>sports</u> as used in this passage means _____.

    A jokes

    B athletic games

    C wears proudly

    D leisure activities

9 The word <u>heretofore</u> means _____.

    A randomly

    B before now

    C by flooding

    D without explanation

10 A <u>likeness</u> is _____.

    A a picture

    B an act of admiration

    C the condition of being liked

    D a person who is similar to another

11 What does <u>discredit</u> mean? Explain your answer.

_____

_____

_____

_____

_____

UNIT 1
Vocabulary Development

Word Relationships

L.7.5, RL.7.4, RI.7.4

Words can have layers of meaning beyond their dictionary definitions. A writer may let you perceive something in an original way by comparing it with something else. He may choose words that appeal to your senses or that create associations in your mind. A writer's choice of words may suggest a relationship with other words that sends your mind in new directions. Or, she may add meaning by including references to familiar stories from history, myth, or other literary works. If you want to understand the points the writer is making, it's important to understand these relationships between words and the ideas behind them.

Figurative Language

Writers use **figurative language** to add beauty, meaning, or force to their words. Some kinds of figurative language are called **imagery,** because of the images they create in your mind. Imagery affects how your senses perceive things. It helps you see, feel, hear, taste, or smell things more vividly. "The room was done up in red and gold velvet" simply tells you how the room was decorated. "It was like being inside a valentine" lets you see the room in a more vivid way. "Someone had painted it in blood and melted butter" suggests the speaker didn't like the room at all.

"It was like being inside a valentine" is one kind of imagery, a **simile.** A simile uses the word *like* or *as* to compare things that are very different from one another. This simile lets you see just how unnaturally red the room looks.

Metaphor is another kind of imagery. It compares two different things without using *like* or *as.* "Someone had painted it in blood and melted butter" is an example of a metaphor. It makes the room feel like an uncomfortable place to be.

Personification is a kind of imagery in which the writer gives human characteristics to some aspect of nature or a human-made object. Read this haiku by the Japanese poet Matsuo Bassho for an example of personification:

> First cold rain pours down
> Even the monkey longs for
> A little straw coat

Symbolism is imagery carried a step further. A symbol in a literary work stands for an idea. For example, a crow may be a symbol of death, a wilted flower a symbol of lost love. Colors are often symbols. Blue may represent sadness, for instance, and gray may represent wisdom.

Figurative language may also add force to words through exaggeration. This is called **hyperbole.** "I've told you a million times to get off Facebook and do your homework!" is an example of hyperbole.

Understatement is the opposite of hyperbole. It adds force to an image by presenting it in a weak way. An example is saying, "It's drizzling a little" when it happens to be raining cats and dogs.

"It's raining cats and dogs" is another kind of figurative language, the **idiom,** or **figurative phrase.** An idiom is a group of words that together mean something entirely different from the individual words. For example, we say that someone comes down with a cold. *Comes down* is an idiom. It doesn't have anything to do with the literal meaning of *comes* or *down*. Figurative phrases like "raining cats and dogs" are sometimes called idioms, too. They are metaphors that have become so common that we don't think of the literal meaning at all.

Allusions are images that are suggested by our culture. Myths are a common source of allusion. For example, someone doing a hard task well is said to be making a "herculean effort," after the Greek hero, Hercules. The Bible is another source of allusions in literature. A person reading about "weather for building an ark," or a football game described as a "David versus Goliath" match-up knows that one describes a heavy rain and the other a team facing a much tougher opponent. Writers often refer to history in their allusions, too. A politician defeated after many terms in office may be said to have "met his Waterloo." This is an allusion to the French general Napoleon, who fought his last (losing) battle at Waterloo in 1815. Literature often alludes to itself. For example, a writer may describe a carefree childhood spent largely outdoors as "a Tom Sawyer upbringing," from the famous character created by Mark Twain.

Elements of Poetry

Imagery is one of the characteristics of **poetry.** It is the tool with which a poet creates images in your mind. A poem is a literary form that is written in **verse:** arrangements of words in lines. A poem's **theme**—the idea that the poet wants you to understand—is often expressed in imagery or symbolism.

Every poem has a **speaker.** The speaker in the poem expresses its ideas and represents the poet's point of view.

There are many different kinds of poems. A **narrative poem** tells a story. A **lyric poem** mainly expresses feelings. Within these categories, there are many kinds of poems. A **sonnet,** for example, is a 14-line lyric poem in a regular rhyming pattern. A **ballad** is a narrative poem originally written to be sung. An **ode** is a lyric poem that expresses noble or enthusiastic feeling and is usually addressed to some person or thing. A **haiku** is a Japanese verse form that contains 17 syllables and is usually about nature. A **limerick** is an English verse form that has five lines and is meant for nonsensical fun.

Many poems have **rhyme**—repeated sounds at the ends of words. Usually the rhyme comes at the ends of a line of poetry, as in this excerpt by Robert Frost:

> *Always the same, when on a faded **night***
> *At last the gathered snow lets down as **white***
> *As may be in dark woods, and with a **song***
> *It shall not make again all winter **long.**...*

Some poems may also have rhyming words in the same line, such as this example by Emily Dickinson:

> *These are the days when the birds come back—*
> *A very **few**—a bird or **two**...*

And many poems have no rhyme at all, as for example, any haiku.

Rhythm is the pattern of stressed or unstressed beats in a line of poetry. A stressed beat has more force than an unstressed beat. Here's a famous example from a sonnet by William Shakespeare:

> *Shall **I** compare thee **to a summer's day?***
> *Thou **are** more **lovely and** more **temperate**...*

Some poems have neither rhyme nor a regular rhythm. Poems like these are called **free verse.** Here is an example by Walt Whitman:

> *The world below the brine,*
> *Forests at the bottom of the sea, the branches and leaves,*
> *Sea-lettuce, vast lichens, strange flowers and seeds, the thick*
> *   tangle, openings, and pink turf...*

Besides using figurative language, poets also add meaning by using the *sounds* of words in playful ways. **Alliteration** is the repetition of the same, or very similar, beginning consonant sounds in a line of poetry. In this line, the /p/ sound is an example of alliteration:

> *Peter, Peter, pumpkin-eater...*

Onomatopoeia is another way that poets play with sound. Words that imitate the sound of something, such as *moo, screech,* and *bang* are examples of onomatopoeia.

A poem may be divided into **stanzas**—groups of lines separated by spaces. The poem that follows is not divided into stanzas.

Guided Practice

Read the poem. Then answer the questions.

To Science

by Edgar Allan Poe

Science! true daughter of Old Time thou art!
Who alterest all things with thy peering eyes.
Why preyest thou thus upon the poet's heart,
Vulture, whose wings are dull realities?
5   How should he love thee? or how deem thee wise?
Who wouldst not leave him in his wandering
To seek for treasure in the jewelled skies,
Albeit he soared with an undaunted wing?
Hast thou not dragged Diana[1] from her car?
10 And driven the Hamadryad[2] from the wood
To seek a shelter in some happier star?
Hast thou not torn the Naiad[3] from her flood,
The Elfin from the green grass, and from me
The summer dream beneath the tamarind tree?

---

[1]Diana: Roman goddess, who carried the moon behind her in a chariot (car)
[2]Hamadryad: mythological spirit, said to live in trees
[3]Naiad: mythological spirit, said to live in streams

Which of the following *best* describes this poem?

A a ballad

B a sonnet

C a limerick

D free verse

This is a 14-line poem with a regular rhyming pattern. It's a sonnet, a form popular in English-language poetry since the 16th century and still being written today. A ballad tells a story. A limerick is a five-line humorous poem, and free verse has no rhyme or regular meter. Choice B is the correct answer.

Determine what form of figurative language the poet *mainly* uses in portraying science.

A idiom

B simile

C metaphor

D personification

Poe portrays science as a daughter of time, which might suggest personification. But in line 4, he compares it to a vulture. That metaphor—a comparison without using *like* or *as*—is consistent with the imagery of wings, peering eyes, and preying upon a poet's heart. The correct answer is choice C.

Determine what poetic device Poe uses in line 11.

A hyperbole

B alliteration

C onomatopoeia

D understatement

In this poem, Poe does not exaggerate (except perhaps in his central image!), understate a point, or use words that represent sounds. The poem does, however, repeat initial sounds for their effect, and not just with the initial /s/ sound in line 11. Choice B is the correct answer.

Interpret the poem. What does the speaker think of science? Explain your answer using images from the poem.

_____

_____

_____

_____

Poe, who is famous for his spooky poems and his tales of mystery and horror, may have had an appreciation for science. However, the speaker in this poem sees it as a bird of prey, feeding on the poet's imagination. Here is a sample answer:

> Poe's speaker calls science a vulture, since poetry is based on metaphor and wonder, and science destroys wonder with its insistence on fact. Science's "peering eyes," he says, are changing everything. A poet can't see spirits in trees anymore, or elves in the grass, because science has destroyed belief in them. Therefore, why should a poet love science, or consider it wise?

Explain the mythological allusions in the poem.

_____

_____

_____

_____

Poe, like many poets, uses figures of Greek and Roman myth as metaphors in this poem. Here is a sample answer:

> Poe uses Diana as a symbol for the moon, and says that science has dragged her from her chariot—by explaining that the moon isn't a goddess at all. He also mentions hamadryads and naiads, spirits of trees and streams, and says that science has driven them to some "happier star," where people maybe still believe in them.

Interpret the poem. What does a vulture symbolize in the poem?

_____

_____

 A vulture is a scavenger, a carrion bird. Poe depicts science as "preying" on a poet's heart, but a bird of prey is a hunter, while a vulture feeds on dead creatures. Here is a sample answer:

> The vulture symbolizes the ripping apart of something once living and beautiful.

In line 4, what does the poet mean by his metaphor of wings?

_____

_____

 The poet imagines the vulture that is science flying on wings that are "dull realities." Here is a sample answer:

> Poe is saying that reality is what makes science "fly," and that reality is boring compared with myth and poetry.

Interpret the poem. What are the jewels referred to in line 7?

_____

 This question asks you to interpret another metaphor. The speaker wants to leave science behind to "seek for treasure in the jeweled sky." What can look like jewels in the sky? Here is a sample answer:

> The jewels referred to in line 7 are "stars."

Word Relationships

When you read "To Science," did you understand the meaning of the words *deem* and *undaunted*, or could you figure them out from context clues? Words like these in isolation can send you to the dictionary. However, if you met them in other contexts, you could probably puzzle out their meaning. Take this sentence, for example: "He considered the book from every aspect, but finally deemed it unsuitable for seventh graders." The sentence tells you that <u>deem</u> is a synonym for "consider," but with a shade of difference. It means, "to consider in a judging way." Or, how about this sentence: "Though undaunted by his epic 4,000-mile journey through wild America, Meriwether Lewis was paralyzed with anxiety when it came to facing down his personal demons." Here you can figure out the meaning of <u>undaunted</u> by **analogy.** The word plainly means the opposite of "paralyzed by anxiety." You can infer that it means something like "courageous," but with a shade of difference. An <u>undaunted</u> person does not *lose* courage or the power to act when faced with danger.

Guided Practice

Read the passage. Then answer the questions.

A King-Sized Gift

by Frank Maltesi

In the spring of 801, an elephant <u>lumbered</u> through the streets of Aachen. Centuries earlier, Aachen had been a Roman fortress; today it is a medium-sized city in western Germany. In 801, it was the capital of the newly crowned Holy Roman Emperor Charles the Great, or Charlemagne. Everyone from the children of the town to the emperor himself came out to see the wondrous beast. It was a gift to Charlemagne from the <u>caliph</u> of Islam, Harun al-Rashid.

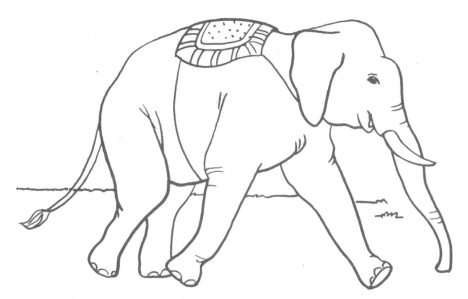

The gift was a result of a remarkable course of diplomacy. Nearly 70 years earlier, Charlemagne's grandfather, Charles Martel, had defeated a Muslim army at the Battle of Tours, in what is now central France. This was the deepest penetration into Christian Europe of the burgeoning Islamic empire. It also marked the limit of the empire's expansion. Only 20 years earlier, Charlemagne himself had led an unsuccessful invasion of Muslim Spain. Now, the two cultures were at peace. The elephant was a token of that peace.

Charlemagne had initiated the negotiations three years earlier by sending an embassy bearing gifts to Baghdad, Harun's capital, a distance of more than 2,000 miles. Harun was also interested in peace. He decided that an elephant was just the thing to impress Charles. The exchange of gifts did not lead to close relations between the two powers, but it did keep the peace. As for the elephant, named Abul Abbas, he became famous across France and Germany. His death in 811 was sadly noted in the official records of Charlemagne's empire.

What is the definition of the word lumbered as used in this passage?

_____

_____

You could substitute the word *walked* or *moved* in that first sentence without changing the meaning much. However, we're talking about an elephant here! Here is a sample answer:

The word lumbered means "moved in a slow and heavy manner"— like an elephant.

A caliph meant something like _____.

A a priest

B a warrior

C an emperor

D a wise ruler

You can figure this one out by analogy. The passage deals with an exchange of gifts between two powerful rulers whose peoples have been at war. You can infer that a caliph (the word actually means "successor" in Arabic) was of equal rank to the emperor Charlemagne. Choice C is the correct answer.

What does the word <u>burgeoning</u> mean in this passage?

The key relationship here is with the word *limit* in the following sentence. The Islamic empire had been <u>burgeoning</u>, but the Battle of Tours marked its limit. Here is a sample answer:

The word <u>burgeoning</u> means "growing or expanding."

Denotation and Connotation

You know that synonyms are words that have almost the same meaning. However, within that "almost" there can be many shades of difference. Consider these two sentences:

Dinner was spaghetti with mushrooms.
Dinner was spaghetti with fungus.

Which of the two plates of spaghetti would you rather eat? You probably know that mushrooms *are* a kind of fungus. However, you think of mushrooms as food, while fungus may suggest rot and ugliness.

The difference is between denotation and connotation. The **denotation** of a word is its dictionary definition. The **connotations** of a word are the associations your feelings and imagination have with it. Connotations can be important whether you're reading poetry or listening to a political speech because they can complicate meaning or plant suggestions in your mind.

Look at this table of synonyms. Think about their connotations. Which word in each group has the most positive connotation for you? Which has the most negative?

- bashful, diffident, reserved, retiring, shy
- firm, obstinate, pig-headed, stubborn, unyielding
- condescending, diplomatic, polite, refined, respectful
- beam, grin, simper, smile, smirk

Guided Practice

Mr. O'Boyle has a 30-year record as a <u>politician</u>.

Mr. O'Boyle has a 30-year record as a <u>statesman</u>.

How do the underlined words change the meaning of the sentence?

_____

_____

 Both <u>politician</u> and <u>statesman</u> denote people who lead public or national affairs. However, <u>politician</u> has a negative connotation that <u>statesman</u> does not have. Here is a sample answer:

A statesman is someone who serves the public and deserves respect. A politician may be serving only himself and his party.

My sister is a <u>cook</u> in that new restaurant.

My sister is a <u>chef</u> in that new restaurant.

How do the underlined words change the meaning of the sentence?

_____

_____

_____

 Both words denote people who prepare food. Their connotations, however, are quite different. Here is a sample answer:

A cook can be anyone who can boil an egg. A chef suggests special training and more interesting meals. You would rather spend your money at a restaurant with a chef than with a cook.

Test Yourself

from **Too Near the Sun**

by Alison Bast

From a thousand feet up, the Palouse was an undulating green carpet with barns and houses tucked into its folds. Driving out to the ridge, I had seen their windows wink at me in the early afternoon sun, as if we were sharing a secret. Now, they showed me their indifferent rooftops. While their eyes kept watch over the wheat fields, mine were on the sky and the far horizon. Hang gliding on such an afternoon, I felt like Icarus's sister. I thoroughly understood how he could have been so giddy and so careless as to meet with that fatal accident. Of course, my wings were aluminum and Mylar, not wax, and I had the advantage of a GPS.

My name is Janine Pierce. I'm a student in biology at Eastern Washington University. My snob family in Seattle doesn't understand why I wanted to go to a cow-town college they and their friends don't respect when I could have gone to a prestigious private college or the main state university back home. One reason was that Cheney is a five-hour drive away from them, so they wouldn't be nagging me to come home every weekend. When I was 18, I would have knocked them both over in my rush to get out the door.

The other reason was hang gliding. From the first time I saw anyone doing it, I knew I had found my sport. The Palouse country, besides being as near to the Garden of Eden as any place I know, is also the hang gliding capital of the universe, or at least of our corner of it. Soaring over the fields, my harness and I as snug a unit as rider and horse, I knew how a hawk must feel circling above the world of people and their trivial affairs. Nevertheless, that world was tugging at me with chains forged of equal parts gravity and responsibility, and there was my truck three-quarters of a mile away.

I made a perfect landing. Then I walked to the truck, dismantled my glider, and stowed it securely. I had just an hour to get home, shower, change, and get to my job waiting tables. Sometimes I felt like the ball in a pinball machine, ricocheting back and forth among classes, work, study, my taciturn roommate Bev who so awkwardly balanced my voluble chatter, and Scott who (just as awkwardly) wanted to be my boyfriend. I threw one last long and longing look at the sky before getting into the truck and starting back toward campus.

1 Determine what type of figurative language Janine uses in the first sentence.

    A   a simile

    B   hyperbole

    C   a metaphor

    D   personification

2 The word <u>undulating</u> means ____.

    A   thick

    B   dirty

    C   wavy

    D   rolled up

3 How does the imagery in the first sentence help you answer question 2?

_____

_____

_____

_____

_____

4 What is Janine alluding to when she says, "I felt like Icarus's sister"? How is this allusion reflected in the title of the story?

_____

_____

_____

_____

_____

5 Janine refers to her "snob" family. Which of these synonyms has the *most* positive connotation?

  A haughty

  B cultured

  C stuck-up

  D highbrow

6 Janine's parents think she has chosen a "cow-town" college. Which of these synonyms has a neutral connotation?

  A hick

  B rural

  C simple

  D unsophisticated

7 What type of figurative language is Janine using when she says, "When I was 18, I would have knocked them both over in my rush to get out the door"?

  A a simile

  B an idiom

  C hyperbole

  D a metaphor

8 What does hang gliding symbolize in this story?

  A freedom

  B childhood

  C fear of dying

  D difficult choices

9 What imagery in the story helps you answer question 8?

_____

_____

_____

_____

_____

10 Analyze the story. What does Janine mean when she says the place she lives in is "as near to the Garden of Eden as any place I know"?

_____

_____

_____

_____

_____

11 How does the sentence about Janine's roommate help you understand the meaning of the words taciturn and voluble?

_____

_____

_____

_____

_____

Content-Specific Words

L.7.6, RI.7.4, RH.7.4, RST.7.4

Your vocabulary consists of several levels of words. First, there are the everyday words you use in conversation. Second, there are the words that you may not use when you speak but that you learn when you read—words like *conjuror, athwart,* and *credence,* such as you encountered in Lesson 1. You might run across words like these in any kind of text, from poetry to history to Internet blogs.

Then there are words that are specific to certain kinds of reading. For example, you wouldn't ordinarily have to understand words like *allele* or *chromosome,* but you would if you were reading about genetics and heredity. *Petroglyph* and *shaman* are not everyday words either. However, if you were reading about certain traditional cultures, you might need to understand them to make sense of what you were reading. Fortunately, you can use context clues to understand these **content-specific words** just as you do when learning any new words.

Guided Practice

Read the passage. Then answer the questions.

Mighty Mitochondria

by Shannon Olsen

When you look at cells under a high-power microscope, it's easy to spot the nucleus and other organelles. Prominent among them are the rod-shaped structures called *mitochondria* (my•toe•CON•dree•uh). Some plant and animal cells contain only one mitochondrion, while human liver and muscle cells have 1,000 to 2,000 each. They are the power plants of living cells. Their main job is to produce a chemical called ATP by combining glucose and other molecules with the oxygen you breathe. ATP is stored in the cells until needed. Then another complicated chemical reaction breaks it down to produce energy for all the cell's needs. Can you see why muscle cells need lots of mitochondria?

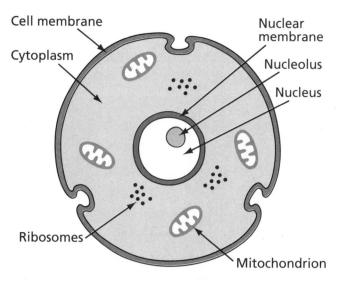

AN ANIMAL CELL

The origins of mitochondria lie far back in the evolution of life on Earth. Their resemblance to the simple cells of prokaryotes has led scientists to conclude that they were once bacteria. As in prokaryotic cells, their DNA is contained in a single, round chromosome. Their genetic code in fact is very similar to that of a major group of bacteria. The current theory is that energy-producing bacteria were in effect eaten by other cells and somehow survived. They then established a symbiotic relationship with the host cells. The host cell provided nutrients, while the bacteria-mitochondria provided energy for the cell's functions. Such a relationship made possible the complex cells of eukaryotes, including all plants and animals. Other organelles may have been incorporated into eukaryotic cells the same way. The chlorophyll-producing chloroplasts of plant cells, for example, resemble a major group of bacteria too.

The theory that mitochondria were originally bacteria was proposed several times by different scientists during the 20th century before it was finally accepted as fact.

Unlike the DNA in the cell nucleus, the DNA in the mitochondria is inherited only through one parent. In humans and other mammals, it is passed along maternally, through egg cells. But in other organisms, such as most evergreen trees, it is inherited paternally, through sperm cells. Just why this should be so is still a scientific mystery.

The word organelles means _____.

   A   organs of the body

   B   small structures within a cell

   C   cells that provide energy to other cells

   D   molecules too small to be seen with a microscope

> Reading the first paragraph, you can understand that organelles can be seen with a microscope, that mitochondria and a nucleus are examples of them, and that they are not cells themselves but are contained within cells. Choice B is the correct answer.

What is the relationship between the words mitochondrion and mitochondria?

> Did you notice that mitochondria are always referred to by the verb *are*, while the word mitochondrion is modified by the word *one?* Here is a sample answer:

Mitochondrion is singular, and mitochondria is plural.

The terms <u>prokaryote</u> and <u>eukaryote</u> refer respectively to ____.

    A   animals and plants

    B   extinct life forms and existing life forms

    C   living things with DNA and those without

    D   living things with simple cells and those with complicated cells

> These Greek-derived terms mean "before nucleus" and "true nucleus." They're used to describe the simple cells of bacteria on the one hand, and the complicated cells of most living things on the other. You can figure this out from the context. All animals and plants have eukaryotic cells; all living things have DNA, and the terms apply to all life forms. The correct answer is choice D.

Write definitions for the other underlined words and phrases in the passage. If you can't tell the meaning of the word from the context, look it up in a print or online dictionary.

glucose   _____

_____

chemical reaction   _____

_____

symbiotic   _____

_____

> Did you get them all? Your answers might read something like these:

    glucose—a simple sugar occurring in plants and animals

    chemical reaction—a process that transforms one set of chemicals into another

    symbiotic—describing an arrangement of two living things that live in cooperation with each other

UNIT 1
Vocabulary Development

Forbidden Music

by Pedro Villareal

The Renaissance (REH•nuh•sahnts) in Europe was a time of cultural flowering. Everyone knows about the great works of painting and sculpture produced during this period by such artists as Leonardo da Vinci and Michelangelo, and the literary works of writers like William Shakespeare in England and Miguel de Cervantes in Spain. Less well known are the musical works of this period, which were part of the development of what is sometimes called classical music. Today, this Renaissance music is heard in special concerts that are usually given in churches. That's only appropriate, since most of the music was originally liturgical, to be performed as part of church services. In fact, one such piece that's often performed today was for years heard in only one church. To perform it elsewhere or even to make copies of the music was forbidden—until a 14-year-old boy let the secret out.

The piece was by an Italian composer named Gregorio Allegri. (Ah•LAY•gree). It was an a capella piece for two choirs, a setting of a Roman Catholic prayer called *Miserere,* from a Latin phrase that means "Have mercy on me, God." Allegri was commissioned to write it in the 1630s by Pope Urban VII. It was to be performed only at a predawn service during Easter week, and only in the Sistine Chapel. This chapel, famous for the frescoes on its walls and ceiling by Michelangelo and other great artists, is in the pope's official palace in Rome. Then as now, it was open to the public and popular among tourists. However, the Allegri *Miserere* was the pope's property. Copying it was forbidden, under penalty of excommunication from the Church. The rule was further enforced by the fact that the *Miserere* was performed in the dark, so that a skilled musician could not transcribe the notes as he or she heard them.

Sistine Chapel

Gregorio Allegri

The ban lasted for more than 130 years, through the reigns of many popes. Then, in 1770, that young boy happened to be in Rome with his father during Easter week. He was an unusually gifted musician whose name was already widely known. Sitting in the chapel that Wednesday morning, he memorized the piece at a single hearing. He wrote down the notes that afternoon in his hotel room. On Good Friday, he went back to the chapel to hear it performed again and to catch any details he may have missed. The boy later sold his manuscript to a music publisher in England. The Allegri *Miserere* was secret no longer.

The boy was summoned to Rome by Pope Clement XIV. However, times had changed. Instead of excommunicating him, the pope praised him for his genius. You probably never have heard of Allegri's *Miserere* before, but you may have heard of the boy who let the secret out. His name was Wolfgang Amadeus Mozart.

1   The term Renaissance describes a period of history most famous for ____.

   A   questioning of authority

   B   a revival of art and learning

   C   the brutal repression of new ideas

   D   the development of new forms of music

2   The word liturgical means ____.

   A   out of date

   B   privately owned

   C   difficult to perform

   D   used in religious worship

3   The musical term a capella means ____.

   A   played for fun

   B   sung without instruments

   C   made up as one goes along

   D   performed at private parties

4 Excommunication means ____.

    A to legally put someone to death

    B to embarrass someone in public

    C to isolate someone from other people

    D to cut someone off from membership in a church

5 What is a commissioned work of art?

_____

_____

_____

_____

_____

6 What are frescoes?

_____

_____

_____

_____

_____

7 What is the relationship between the words transcribe and manuscript, and what do they mean?

_____

_____

_____

_____

_____

REVIEW

Vocabulary Development

Read the poem. Then answer the questions.

Nonsense Rhyme

by Elinor Wylie

Whatever's good or bad or both
Is surely better than the none
There's grace in either love or loathe
Sunlight, or freckles on the sun.

5 The worst and best are both inclined
To snap like vixens at the truth
But, O beware the middle mind
That purrs and never shows a tooth!

Beware the smooth ambiguous smile
10 That never pulls the lips apart
Salt of pure and pepper of vile
Must season the extremer heart.

A pinch of fair, a pinch of foul
And bad and good make best of all
15 Beware the moderated soul
That climbs no fractional inch to fall.

Reason's a rabbit in a hutch,
And ecstasy's a were-wolf ghost
But, O beware the nothing much
20 And welcome madness and the most!

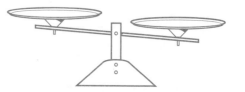

1 This poem is *best* described as ____.

 A a ballad

 B a sonnet

 C free verse

 D a lyric poem

2 The word relationships in line 3 suggest that loathe means ____.

 A hate

 B wicked

 C support

 D understand

3 Interpret the meaning of the metaphor in line 17.

_____

_____

_____

_____

_____

4 Determine what type of imagery the poet uses in line 7.

 A idiom

 B simile

 C metaphor

 D personification

5 Words like snap (line 6) and purrs (line 8) are examples of ____.

 A hyperbole

 B alliteration

 C onomatopoeia

 D understatement

6 In line 9, what does the word <u>ambiguous</u> mean?

   A false

   B reassuring

   C anxious to please

   D not having a clear meaning

7 Determine which meaning the word <u>pinch</u> has in line 13.

   A to steal

   B a small amount

   C the act of squeezing sharply

   D to squeeze between the thumb and forefinger

8 Interpret the poem. What does the imagery of salt and pepper mean in line 11?

_____

_____

_____

_____

_____

9 In line 7, what does the word <u>middle</u> connote to the speaker? Explain why, considering the imagery in the poem.

_____

_____

_____

_____

_____

UNIT 1
Vocabulary Development

Writing Without an Alphabet

by Victor Chinn

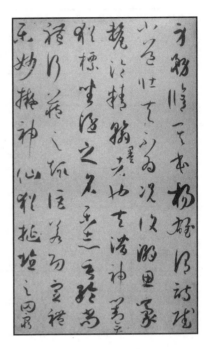

How can you organize a dictionary in alphabetical order if you don't have an alphabet? That is one of the "great walls" separating those of us in the West from an understanding of the Chinese language. The Chinese might just as well ask the question, "How can an English speaker possibly read books written 600 years ago when spelling and pronunciation have changed so completely?"

The questions are two sides of the same coin. Written Chinese started out as a logographic language, like the hieroglyphics of the ancient Egyptians. Instead of standing for a sound, each symbol represented a word. Each logogram was originally a picture. Over the centuries, they became more abstract. They came to represent ideas rather than words, and two or more symbols would be combined to express new ideas. By the time of Confucius, around 500 B.C., written Chinese was basically the same as it is today. Since then, Chinese pronunciation has become greatly simplified, and the language has diverged into many separate dialects. No modern Chinese could understand Confucius's spoken language if he were suddenly to turn up to give a lecture on TV. However, his *writings* are readily understandable to anyone who can read, because the symbols and their meanings have not changed.

Chinese lexicography goes way back in China's history. Scholars were compiling dictionaries of the language even before Confucius. They recorded words with unusual meanings from different parts of the land and incorporated them into the written language. The earliest Chinese dictionaries were tables of synonyms, more like what we would call a thesaurus. Later ones organized logograms by *radicals,* the basic components that were combined to make up more complicated logograms. They were arranged in order of the number and order of brush strokes needed to write each logogram. Other dictionaries were organized by rhymes. Many modern Chinese dictionaries compromise by organizing words alphabetically according to the way they are transliterated into our alphabet, together with an index of radicals.

Obviously, none of these methods is as simple as listing words in alphabetical order. On the other hand, have you ever tried reading a book in English as it was spoken and written 600 years ago?

10 To what is the author alluding in the second sentence of the passage? What does he mean by this allusion?

_____

_____

_____

_____

_____

11 In paragraph 2, what does the figurative phrase "two sides of the same coin" mean?

_____

_____

_____

_____

_____

12 The root logo comes from the Greek word for *word*. What does logographic mean? Explain why.

_____

_____

_____

_____

_____

13 A sentence that is transliterated is _____.

   A put into the words of another language

   B put into the writing system of another language

   C explained according to word-by-word definitions

   D explained according to the meaning of the whole sentence

Key Ideas and Details

How many different kinds of things have you read this week? Perhaps, you've read an exciting novel or an inspiring poem. Maybe, you're going to be in a class play and are reading the script. You might have read an article about science on the Internet or an editorial in the newspaper. You may have gotten information you need for your daily life from a bus schedule or a movie listing. Whatever you read, you're absorbing ideas and details and making connections among them in your mind. You need to be able to remember those details, to identify the most important ones, and to understand how they relate to one another.

This unit is about those ideas and details that make up the fabric of a text.

● **In Lesson 4,** you'll learn about noting details and remembering them accurately to understand and explain what a text means. You'll learn how to identify details that are stated directly in a text and those that may take some figuring out. And you'll learn how to identify the evidence that supports your understanding of the details.

● **Lesson 5** is about the ideas that are supported by the details. You'll learn how to identify the most important ideas that a text is about and how they are developed over the course of the text. And you'll learn how to summarize a text—to explain briefly what it's about, referring only to the most important ideas and details.

● **Lesson 6** is about the connections between ideas and details in literary texts. You learned something about the elements of poetry in Lesson 2. In this lesson, you'll learn about the elements of stories and plays. You'll learn how to identify key details about the characters, events, and settings in a literary text and how they interconnect with one another to tell a story. And you'll learn how these key elements influence one another in ways that move the story along and make it seem more real.

● **Lesson 7** is about the connections between ideas and details in informational texts. Just as characters, events, and places work together to tell a story, so do people, events, and ideas relate to one another to give you insights about subjects such as historical events or discoveries in science. You'll learn how to recognize these connections and to use them to better understand what you're reading about.

Understanding a Text

RL.7.1, RI.7.1, RST.7.1

Vocabulary
adjacent
conflated
countenance
despot
perfidy

No matter what you read, whether it's fiction, an article about history, or even the listing for a movie you want to see, being able to accurately recall details and to find evidence for them is the first step in understanding a text.

Guided Practice

Read the poem. Then answer the questions.

God's Judgment on a Wicked Bishop

by Robert Southey

The summer and autumn had been so wet,
That in winter the corn was growing yet,
'Twas a piteous sight to see all around
The grain lie rotting on the ground.

5 Every day the starving poor
Crowded around Bishop Hatto's door,
For he had a plentiful last-year's store,
And all the neighborhood could tell
His granaries were furnish'd well.

10 At last Bishop Hatto appointed a day
To quiet the poor without delay;
He bade them to his great Barn repair,
And they should have food for the winter there.

Rejoiced such tidings good to hear,
15 The poor folk flock'd from far and near;
The great barn was full as it could hold
Of women and children, and young and old.

Then when he saw it could hold no more,
Bishop Hatto he made fast the door;
20 And while for mercy on Christ they call,
He set fire to the Barn and burnt them all.

UNIT 2 ✖✖✖✖✖✖✖✖✖✖✖✖✖✖✖✖✖✖✖✖✖✖✖✖✖✖✖✖✖✖✖✖✖✖✖✖✖
Key Ideas and Details

"I' faith 'tis an excellent bonfire!" quoth he,
"And the country is greatly obliged to me,
For ridding it in these times forlorn
25   Of Rats that only consume the corn."

So then to his palace returned he,
And he sat down to supper merrily,
And he slept that night like an innocent man;
But Bishop Hatto never slept again.

30   In the morning as he enter'd the hall
Where his picture hung against the wall,
A sweat like death all over him came,
For the Rats had eaten it out of the frame.

As he look'd there came a man from his farm—
35   He had a countenance[1] white with alarm;
"My Lord, I open'd your granaries this morn,
And the Rats had eaten all your corn."

Another came running presently,
And he was pale as pale could be,
40   "Fly! my Lord Bishop, fly," quoth he,
"Ten thousand Rats are coming this way,…
The Lord forgive you for yesterday!"

"I'll go to my tower on the Rhine," replied he,
"'Tis the safest place in Germany;
45   The walls are high and the shores are steep,
And the stream is strong and the water deep."

Bishop Hatto fearfully hasten'd away,
And he crost the Rhine without delay,
And reach'd his tower, and barr'd with care
50   All the windows, doors, and loopholes there.

He laid him down and closed his eyes;…
But soon a scream made him arise,
He started and saw two eyes of flame
On his pillow from whence the screaming came.

55   He listen'd and look'd;… it was only the Cat;
And the Bishop he grew more fearful for that,
For she sat screaming, mad with fear
At the Army of Rats that were drawing near.

For they have swum over the river so deep,
60   And they have climb'd the shores so steep,
And up the Tower their way is bent,
To do the work for which they were sent.

[1]countenance: face

They are not to be told by the dozen or score,
By thousands they come, and by myriads and more,
65 Such numbers had never been heard of before,
Such a judgment had never been witness'd of yore.

Down on his knees the Bishop fell,
And faster and faster his beads did he tell,
As louder and louder drawing near
70 The gnawing of their teeth he could hear.

And in at the windows and in at the door,
And through the walls helter-skelter they pour,
And down from the ceiling and up through the floor,
From the right and the left, from behind and before,
75 From within and without, from above and below,
And all at once to the Bishop they go.

They have whetted their teeth against the stones,
And now they pick the Bishop's bones:
They gnaw'd the flesh from every limb,
80 For they were sent to do judgment on him!

Analyze the poem. Why were the poor starving?

   A   Rats had eaten their crops.

   B   They had been lazy all summer.

   C   Bad weather had ruined the crops.

   D   The king had seized the food for his army.

The first stanza tells how the grain was rotting. Nothing suggests that the people had been lazy, and there is no mention of a king. As for the rats, they come later. Choice C is the correct answer.

Why did the poor crowd around Bishop Hatto's door?

   A   They knew he had food.

   B   He was the ruler of the area.

   C   He had a reputation for kindness.

   D   They wanted him to pray for them.

The second stanza tells that everyone knew the bishop had grain stored. He may have been the ruler, but he was not kind, and the peasants were not asking for his prayers. The correct answer is choice A.

Determine when the legend narrated in the poem took place.

A around 500 B.C.

B around A.D. 1000

C around A.D. 1800

D in the present day

The poem tells you that the story takes place in Germany, but not when. To answer the question, you have to **make an inference** based on evidence in the poem combined with what you already know. Plainly, this is a legend of long ago, certainly not the present day, and well before 1800 (which was about when Southey wrote the poem). There were no bishops or Christians B.C., and the events suggest Europe's era of knights, castles, and Robin Hood. The answer is choice B.

According to the legend, what were the rats that overran the tower? What evidence in the poem supports your answer?

_____

_____

A literal reading of the poem simply tells you that the rats were rats. However, look closely at line 25, where the wicked bishop describes the peasants as "Rats that only consume the corn." Here is a sample answer:

> The rats were the souls of the people the bishop murdered. The
> evidence is that he called them rats, and that night the rats came.

The Legend of the Mouse Tower

by Frank Maltesi

Visitors to Germany are charmed by the quaint ruined castles that dot the landscape and the legends attached to them. No medieval structure draws as much attention from the tourists as the *Mäusethurm,* or "mouse tower," that stands on a rock in the River Rhine near the city of Bingen. For it was here that the wicked Bishop Hatto was allegedly gnawed to death by mice as punishment for his ghastly slaughter of the peasants during a famine in the year 970. According to the legend, he herded the starving poor into a barn under the pretext of giving them food, and then had his servants set it on fire. As it burned, he is supposed to have said, "They are like mice, only good to devour the corn"—hence the nature of his punishment. It's a grim little moral tale, but of course it is pure myth.

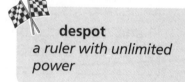

See where the story takes place. Find the locations and photographs of the German cities of Bingen and Mainz in a print or online atlas.

There were actually two bishops named Hatto, both well attested to in German chronicles. Hatto I, Archbishop of Mainz, was a maker of kings in his turbulent time and a power behind the throne. There is no indication that he was crueler to the poor than any despot of his or any other era. However, he was despised for his ruthlessness and perfidy for having had a rival to his candidate for the throne beheaded after solemnly pledging his safety as an official of the church. Hatto I died in May 913. Almost immediately, legends began to circulate about his death. One said that he was struck by lightning, another that he was dropped into a volcano by the devil.

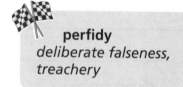

despot
a ruler with unlimited power

perfidy
deliberate falseness, treachery

Hatto II, about whom the Mouse Tower legend arose, was archbishop from 968 to 970. He had a different sort of reputation in his lifetime. He had been the able abbot of a monastery in a different part of Germany, where he built a church on an island in the lake. Famines occurred regularly, and the poor suffered, but there is no record of Hatto ever deliberately murdering any. The famine behind the legend may actually have taken place in 974 or 977, after Hatto was dead. As for his *"Mäusethurm* on the Rhine," it did not exist during his time. The Romans had built a tower there, but it had long since vanished. Some time after 1200, Archbishop Siegfried II built a new one for the purpose of collecting taxes on the goods that passed along the river. The German word *Maus* or *Mauth* means "toll." No tax is ever popular, but a toll collected on grain is especially hard on the poor.

It is easy to see how the legends could have become conflated. Indeed, similar tales involving cruel bishops, kings, counts, and dukes are told from England to Denmark to Switzerland to Poland. In some of them, the ruler starves the poor in a dungeon; in others, he poisons them. However, the rat or mouse element is always the same. As for the *Mäusethurm*, it was destroyed in 1689, during a war. The present one that tourists come to see was built as a lighthouse barely 150 years ago.

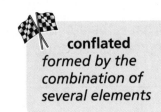

conflated
formed by the combination of several elements

According to the article, the Mouse Tower legend arose from an event in the year _____.

A 913

B 970

C 977

D 1200

Precise dates are useful in separating history from fiction. Bishop Hatto II, who supposedly perished in the Mouse Tower, died in 970, and you could look it up. Choice B is the correct answer.

One reason the date of Hatto's death is important to understanding the facts behind the legend is that _____.

A there was no "Mouse Tower" at the time

B famines were unfortunately frequent at the time

C the first Bishop Hatto actually lived much earlier

D there are many accounts of the legend from different places

The author leaves it up to you to draw some conclusions. All the answer choices are factual, according to the article. However, if Bishop Hatto lived in the 10th century, and the tower wasn't built until the 13th, that pretty much proves that things didn't happen anything like Southey's poem says they did. The correct answer is choice A.

What is the author's basis for stating that neither Bishop Hatto deliberately murdered peasants?

_____

_____

_____

✓ From what you know of history, it's perfectly reasonable to believe that a powerful ruler *could* have been cruel enough to herd peasants into a barn and set it on fire. However, according to the article, the careers of both bishops are "well attested to." Here is a sample answer:

There are records in Germany of both bishops Hatto. They say that Hatto I was a bad guy in some ways, but there is nothing to suggest that Hatto II was so cruel.

Based on details in the article, how might the legend of the Mouse Tower arisen?

_____

_____

_____

_____

_____

_____

✓ The article shows how several legends could have become conflated, or combined into one story. There are a lot of details that suggest how this might have happened. Here is a sample answer:

There was a later tower that was called a toll tower, and the name could have come to be called "mouse tower" because the German words are similar. The tower had a bad reputation among the poor because of the taxes collected there. There were frequently famines, and a memory of a Bishop Hatto who had done something bad. The story of the wicked ruler eaten by rats or mice was so widespread that it may have been a folktale. All these facts could have been mixed together to create the legend.

UNIT 2 ▨▨▨▨▨▨▨▨▨▨▨▨▨▨▨▨▨▨▨▨▨▨▨▨
Key Ideas and Details

Test Yourself

adjacent
beside or next to

What Happens When You Make a Cell Phone Call?

by Einar F. Klamst

When Martin Cooper invented the cell phone, in 1973, it weighed two pounds and could do only one thing: make phone calls. Imagine lugging it around in your pocket! Today's cell phones, besides being much smaller, let you store phone numbers, surf the Internet, keep an appointment schedule, play games, do math calculations, take pictures, and of course, send text messages. It's no wonder more and more people are giving up their stodgy old "land-line" phones altogether.

A cell phone is actually a two-way radio. It has more in common with walkie-talkies and CB radios than with the telephone invented by Alexander Graham Bell in 1876. That type of phone converts your voice to electric signals that are carried by wires to a receiving unit, which converts them back into sound waves. A cell phone, by contrast, transmits a radio signal over a certain frequency. A broadcast radio station typically has thousands of watts of power and transmits over one frequency—97.6 FM, for example. If more than one station that powerful were broadcasting over the same frequency in the same area, you'd hear a jumble of noise, like at a crowded party. A cell phone uses low power, 0.6 or three watts, so many people can use the same frequency at once. A walkie-talkie or CB radio also operates on low power. That's why it has a range of only a few miles. So, how can your cell phone communicate with other phones all over the world?

That's where the **cells** come in. Each cell-phone service region is divided into hexagonal cells that fit together like a honeycomb. Each cell measures about ten square miles. Each cell has a **base station.** It consists of the familiar cellular tower, which is actually a radio antenna, with transmitting and receiving equipment at its base.

When you turn on your cell phone, it sends a signal along a control channel to the nearest base station. The station identifies your phone from a code that's programmed in. When you make a call, the base station "knows" who's calling. It assigns a voice channel to you and the person you call. Unlike a walkie-talkie, a cell-phone **voice channel** uses two frequencies, so that both of you can talk at once. Today's cell phones can typically handle more than 1,500 frequencies, so the tower finds a pair that no one else in the cell is using. When your phone and the tower switch on these frequencies, your call is connected.

Two cell-phone users may be assigned the same frequency at the same time if they are not in adjacent cells. As long as you and your phone remain stationary, this is not a problem. However, suppose you're talking to a friend while riding on a bus? As the bus nears the edge of your cell, the base station senses that your signal is weakening. At the same time, the base station in the adjacent cell senses that it is strengthening. The two stations communicate with each other over a control channel. As you pass between cells, your phone gets a signal to change frequencies and is switched to the new cell. This hand-off usually occurs so smoothly that you don't even notice it.

What if you're not calling a friend on another cell phone but leaving a message for your mom at home? The base center in your cell knows that the number you're calling is a land-line phone. It automatically switches control of your call to a central station that handles such connections and controls all the nearby base stations.

1 According to the article, a cell phone is most like _____.

   A a two-way radio

   B a land-line telephone

   C a broadcast radio station

   D a system of signal towers

UNIT 2
Key Ideas and Details

2 According to the article, a cell-phone system in a big city will have ____.

    A   one voice channel for every phone

    B   about 1,500 available cell-phone frequencies

    C   one base center for every cell-phone company

    D   one cell-phone tower for every 10 square miles

3 What are two main differences between a cell phone and a walkie-talkie, and what are the reasons for them?

_____

_____

_____

_____

4 What would happen if a system problem caused two or more calls in a cell to be assigned the same frequency?

_____

_____

_____

_____

5 Suppose you call a friend on your cell phone but can't get a connection until you have tried two or three times. Based on information from the article, what might the problem be?

_____

_____

_____

_____

UNIT 2
Key Ideas and Details

57

Main Idea and Summaries

RL.7.2, RI.7.2, RH.7.2, RST.7.2

Vocabulary

abecedarians

immuring

obstinate

Everything you read has a **main idea** or a **theme**—something that answers the basic question "What's it about?" Identifying that main idea, and the most important ideas that support it, is one of the most important reading skills. Once you know what you're reading about, the details all seem to fall into place. The main ideas of each section or chapter are details that support the main ideas of the work as a whole. The main ideas of each paragraph are details that support the section. If you've understood what you've read, you should be able to write a summary that briefly answers that key question, "What's it about?"

Guided Practice

Read the story. Then answer the questions.

I'll Die Screaming

by Karen Stamfil

"We got horror," my brother said. "Ask Mom to get down to Gresham's before it closes and buy some fake blood. A lot of it. Please. We'll be back in half an hour."

"Okay," I said, but Michael had already hung up. I had a feeling that the next 48 hours were going to be a horror show, but not necessarily in the way he intended.

My brother has wanted to be a filmmaker ever since I can remember. When I was 5 and he was 9, he had me acting in backyard productions. He directed and shot them with our family video camera and edited them on a computer. Since then he'd made more than a dozen short films, but he'd never done anything like the 48-Hour Film Project before.

"It's an international competition," he had explained weeks earlier. I was looking over his shoulder as he signed up for the project online. "Everyone's given the same character, prop, and line of dialogue to work into a movie. Then you draw a genre from a hat, and you have to write, shoot, and edit a four- to seven-minute film and get it to contest headquarters within 48 hours."

"What's a zhon-ruh?"

"It means the kind of movie, like comedy or action or musical."

Many locations have moviemaking contests for students your age, for which all you may need is a simple digital camcorder or even a cell phone. Use the Internet to find out whether any such events take place in your area.

UNIT 2 ▨▨▨▨▨▨▨▨▨▨▨▨▨▨▨▨▨▨▨▨▨▨▨▨▨
Key Ideas and Details

"Why can't you just say 'kind' then?"

"Because it's 'genre,'" Michael said. "And because I'm a nice brother, I'm going to let you be part of my crew, and maybe even have a part in the film."

An hour earlier, before Michael and his chief assistants Tommy and Ron had driven down to contest headquarters to get their "genre" assignment, the cast and crew had assembled in our living room, nine or ten of them. They were fortifying themselves for the 48 hours ahead on the pizza and soda Mom had provided.

"I hope we get horror," Michael was saying. "We can shoot in Tommy's basement. That place has been giving me the creeps since I was 6."

Tommy Holton has been Michael's best friend forever. "Yeah, like that time you were convinced there were aliens down there, and that spider you thought was as big as your head," he said.

Michael threw a pillow at him. "It was the way that spotlight cast its shadow," he said. "If we do get horror, I hope that spider is still down there. I know how to light it now to make it *really* big."

"What if we get something weird, like western?" Laura Ramirez said. She was one of the students Michael had recruited from the high-school drama club.

"Well, then, somebody will have to be the horse," Michael said, looking at me. "And my sister Isabel can be the back end."

A few of Michael's friends had the good grace not to laugh. I knew very well that as a seventh grader among high-school kids, I wasn't going to be playing the lead. That was cool. I was happy to be included in the project (I thought) and was looking forward to the adventure (sort of).

Now, the adventure was about to begin. I didn't know whether the horror was going to be aliens or giant spiders, but I knew what I was going to be. The screamer. The hapless victim. The one who was going to spend a lot of time on the floor of Tommy Holton's basement, wearing the fake blood Mom was buying at Gresham's Novelty Shop.

Determine which sentence describes what the story is mainly about.

A   A group of teens make a movie.

B   A girl takes part in her brother's movie project.

C   Something scary happens in the basement of a house.

D   A high-school student enters a filmmaking competition.

Despite it's title, you know that this is more likely to be a funny story than a scary story. A group of teens making a movie in 48 hours may be what *happens* in the story (the plot), however, what the story is *about* (the theme) has more to do with Isabel than her brother and his friends, or the contest. She's telling the story. You can predict that she's going to have a bigger role to play than as victim in her brother's movie. Choice B is the correct answer.

How is Isabel's role in the story developed over the course of this text?

_____

_____

_____

_____

_____

You can already see the theme developing—the younger sister whom the older brother condescendingly includes in his project. Any guesses as to who's going to save the day? Here is a sample answer:

Isabel starts out by suggesting that things are not going to go entirely smoothly on this movie set. She's being *allowed* to participate, as if Michael is doing her a big favor. She thinks she's going to end up playing the victim, but she also hints of the adventure to come, and you can infer that she's going to be an active participant.

Which of these sentences expresses the main idea of paragraph 2?

A   My brother has wanted to be a filmmaker ever since I can remember.

B   When I was 5 and he was 9, he had me acting in his backyard productions.

C   He directed and shot them with our family video camera and edited them on a computer.

D   Since then he'd made more than a dozen short films, but he'd never done anything like the 48-Hour Film Project before.

The **topic sentence** expresses the main idea of the paragraph. All the sentences support or explain the main idea: that Michael wants to make movies when he grows up. The correct answer is choice A.

What function does paragraph 4 have in the story?

_____

_____

This paragraph (indeed, this whole part of the story) serves as **exposition**: It introduces the characters and situation and hints at the conflict to come. Here is a sample answer:

Paragraph 4 explains what the 48-Hour Film Project is, which you need to know to understand the events of the story.

Write a summary of the passage.

_____

_____

A summary is a short restatement of the ideas in a passage. It is not a review. It should include only the main ideas and the most important supporting details. Here is a sample answer:

Isabel's brother is leading a team in a contest to make a movie in 48 hours. He's letting Isabel take part in the project, which will be a horror film. From the way he teases her, she thinks she's going to be cast as the victim.

Two Incidents on Empire Boulevard

by Kayla Owens

It was the week of my daughter's wedding, D-day minus three. Guests had been arriving since the previous weekend, and I'd been juggling my job with playing hostess and mother-of-the-bride. This was my morning for errands: to the bakery, to the caterer, to Clodagh's Alterations to pick up Denise's wedding gown. I could feel the tension throughout my body as I inched along Empire Boulevard. That was before the car died on me.

There I was, stuck in the middle of the busiest road in the North End, drivers glaring and beeping their horns, my insides twisted in knots, wishing that Denise and Mark had decided to elope. Fortunately, a nice police officer happened by. He stopped traffic and helped me get my car to the curb until the tow truck came. That seemed to take six hours, but it was probably only one. They towed my car to a repair garage and got me a rental; I phoned everyone to tell them I'd be late, and got on with my busy day.

Later that afternoon, I was heading home, exhausted. I found myself once again on Empire Boulevard. I was stopped at a traffic light when there came a tap at the passenger-side window. I looked up, startled. There was a homeless man in a dirty gray coat, gaunt, bearded—you've seen him before, though you probably avoided looking at him very closely, same as I had. I sighed, took a couple dollars from my purse, opened the window, and handed it to him. He muttered something that might have been "Thank You," but he didn't stop there. He launched into an involved explanation of his life and how he'd come to be in such a state. I wondered whether the light was ever going to turn green. "Please," I said, cutting him off. "I'm having a very bad day."

The homeless man took a step back. He looked at me incredulously. "You're having a bad day?" he said. *"You're* having a bad day?? Lady, *look at me!"*

Then the light changed, and I was outathere.

You see people like that in every city. They all have their own story. Thinking of what his life must be like didn't make my bad day any better. Yet that Sunday, amid all the wedding festivities and joy, my mind couldn't help coming back to that man and when the last time might have been that he'd had anything to be joyous about.

UNIT 2
Key Ideas and Details

Which of these sayings *best* expresses the main theme of this essay?

A   Every "you" is an "I."

B   A smile is only a frown turned upside down.

C   The grass is always greener on the other side of the fence.

D   I had no shoes and complained, until I met a man who had no feet.

The author is comparing two incidents: that put her own problems in perspective. Her thoughts aren't about considering others as individuals or looking on the bright side. They're about recognizing that some people's troubles are a lot worse than her own. Choice D is the answer you want.

What is a secondary theme that the author develops in her essay?

_____

Until the homeless man enters the narrative, the essay is all about the author. Here is a sample answer:

Family celebrations can be stressful for the family.

How does the author develop her themes over the course of the text?

_____

_____

_____

_____

 This question is asking you to analyze how the author reveals the main ideas to you, the reader. Here is a sample answer:

> At first, the theme seems to be about the author and how a joyous occasion is turning out to be one hassle after another. Then, she introduces the homeless man, and you realize that the main idea isn't about her troubles at all. Even on her daughter's wedding day, she's thinking about the poor man on the street.

Which of these sentences is *best* left out of a summary of the passage?

A   The author's car breaks down on a busy street.

B   The author's daughter has a joyous wedding after all.

C   The author realizes that her problems are not so terrible.

D   The author is in a rush to do errands for her daughter's wedding.

 A summary should include only the main ideas and the most important details that support them. Choices A, C, and D are all important to understanding the themes. However, the essay is not about the wedding, it's about the two incidents on Empire Boulevard and the author's feelings about them. The correct answer is choice B.

Test Yourself

obstinate
stubborn

School Days, 1800

Adapted from The School District As It Was, *by Warren Burton (1833)*

The Old School-house in District No. 5, stood on the top of a very high hill, on the north side of what was called the County road... Here was the center of the district, as near as the surveyor's chain could designate. The people east would not permit the building to be carried one rod further west, and those of the opposite quarter were as obstinate on their side. So, here it was placed; and this continued to be literally the "hill of science" to generation after generation of learners for 50 years…

We will now go inside…. A door on the left admits us to the schoolroom. Here is a space about 20 feet long and 10 wide, the reading and spelling parade. At…the left as you enter, was one seat and writing bench, making a right angle with the rest of the seats. This was occupied in the winter by two of the oldest males in the school. At the opposite end was the [teacher's] desk, raised upon a platform a foot from the floor. The fireplace was on the right, halfway between the door of entrance and another leading into a dark closet, where the girls put their outside garments and their dinner baskets. This also served as a fearful dungeon for the immuring of offenders. Directly opposite the fireplace was an aisle, two feet and a half wide, running up an inclined floor to the opposite side of the room. On each side of this were five or six long seats and writing benches, for the accommodation of the school at their studies. In front of these, next to the spelling floor, were low narrow seats for abecedarians and others near that rank. In general, the older the scholar, the farther from the front his location….

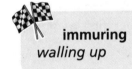

immuring
walling up

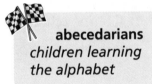

abecedarians
children learning the alphabet

The severest duty I was ever called to perform was sitting on that little front seat, at my first winter school. My lesson… conveyed no ideas, excited no interest, and, of course, occupied but very little of my time. There was nothing before me on which to lean my head, or lay my arms, but my own knees. I could not lie down to drowse, as in summer, for want of room on the crowded seat. How my limbs ached for the freedom and activity of play!… But these bonds upon my limbs were not all. I had trials by fire in addition. Every cold forenoon, the old fireplace, wide and deep, was kept a roaring furnace of flame, for the benefit of blue noses, chattering jaws and aching toes, in the more distant regions. The end of my seat, just opposite the chimney, was cozy with melting pitch, and sometimes almost smoked with combustion….

1 What two themes does Warren Burton explore in this essay?

_____

_____

_____

_____

2 How does Burton make you experience the school of 1800 over the course of the essay?

_____

_____

_____

_____

3 What is the main idea that Burton wants you to take away from the first paragraph?

   A Science was the main subject taught at the school.

   B The schoolhouse was in the exact center of the town.

   C The school was in use long after it should have been replaced.

   D The location of the schoolhouse was determined by town politics.

4 Write a summary of the essay.

_____

_____

_____

_____

_____

UNIT 2
Key Ideas and Details

Literary Elements

RL.7.3

Vocabulary

Athena
claustrophobic
exemplary
franchise
Muse
onus
paraphernalia
Poseidon
subordinates

All narratives, whether in the form of a story, poem, or play, include characters, events, and a setting. How these elements interact with one another make the story livelier and your reading more interesting.

Elements of a Narrative

Any story will feature **characters.** The ways they think, feel, and respond to one another and to challenges are what move the story forward. An author makes characters seem real through descriptions of the way they look, act, and talk. The talk is called **dialogue.** Sometimes the *way* a character talks can be as important as what he says. It can tell you where the character comes from, where he fits in his social world, the face he presents to other people, and the face he keeps private.

You can learn about characters in stories by what they do and say. You can also learn about the characters from what other characters and the author say about them.

The events of the story make up the plot. A **plot** unfolds as a series of episodes as characters respond to the events. Episodes usually take place in chronological order, but they are not always told that way. Part of the story may be told in flashback, narrating events that happened earlier.

The element of the plot that makes a story exciting is the **conflict.** Sometimes the conflict is a struggle between two or more characters. It may also be an inner conflict, such as a character choosing whether or not to take a dangerous risk in order to do what he thinks is right. It may be a conflict between a character and the events, such as a person struggling to complete a task despite obstacles. Or, it may involve the setting, as when a character has to cope with life in a new city.

Any plot will have an **inciting incident,** which sets the conflict in motion. In Mark Twain's *The Adventures of Tom Sawyer,* for instance, the inciting incident is Tom and Huck's witnessing of the murder in the graveyard. Most of the plot consists of **rising action,** which continues until you know how the conflict will turn out. That point is called the **climax.** In *Tom Sawyer,* the climax comes when Tom and Becky are rescued from the cave. The **falling action** is made up of the events that follow the climax and that happen as a result of it. It includes a **resolution** explaining what happens to the characters. A resolution may take several chapters to conclude, as in *Tom Sawyer.* Or, it may be as simple as "And they lived happily ever after."

The **setting** is the time and place in which events of the story take place. The time can be past, present, or future. An author uses the setting to create the **tone,** or feeling of the story, and to provide a background against which the characters interact. Often, the events of the plot change, the setting, as when a character is forced by sudden circumstances to leave her country home and seek a job in a strange city. The setting and the way characters respond to it can be an important part of the story's outcome.

The setting helps shape the characters and determine the choices they make. Sometimes the setting almost becomes a character in itself. And the events of the plot and the way characters respond to them can change the setting.

Review the first part of the story "I'll Die Screaming" on pages 58 and 59 before reading the next passage, from later in the story. Use what you learn from both parts of the story to answer the questions.

Guided Practice

Read the story. Then answer the questions.

I'll Die Screaming (continued)

by Karen Stamfil

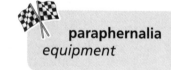

claustrophobic
afraid of being in an enclosed space

Tommy's basement *was* creepy. It made my skin itch just to be there, and with eight people and all the equipment crammed in, I was feeling claustrophobic. Michael and his A-team had obviously been busy while the rest of us were sleeping. I don't know how much of the effect was natural to the place and how much was due to the stuff that Michael had placed there among the rough, low beams, pipes, bare light bulbs, cobwebs, and tools. A three-foot-long saw leaned against one wall, its fangs bared menacingly. Rickety shelves held dusty bottles of interestingly colored liquids. An unmade cot rested in one corner. The wall beside it was pasted with newspaper clippings that looked old but that someone had mocked up on a computer. Then there was the movie paraphernalia Michael had rented: bright lights in black metal cabinets, a microphone at the end of a long pole, and the professional-model camera. And mirrors. Every movable mirror from our house was there, including the one from my bedroom. For some reason, the script they had written had a lot to do with mirrors. Maybe Michael thought they were scary. At one point I was supposed to fall against a mirror and shatter it with my forehead—not for real; Michael was going to do something tricky to make it look authentic—and then he would stop the camera, and out would come the fake blood.

paraphernalia
equipment

"I want to block the fight scene first," Michael said. "That's going to be the hardest to film because of the different angles. Then we'll rehearse the other scenes, and hopefully we'll start shooting after lunch." He looked at his watch and then at Tommy. "You hear from Ron?"

UNIT 2
Key Ideas and Details

"Negative," Tommy said. "I've been leaving messages for him all morning."

Michael muttered something. "Ron's not a flake. He wouldn't have left his sound equipment here if he wasn't coming back."

I cleared my throat. "I think I might know what happened to him."

Everyone looked at me. "Isabel, what would you know about it?" Michael said.

I told him about the call from Ron's mom. "She thought he was with you all night. I think she was mad that he wasn't."

"Uh-oh," Tommy said.

"He said he was going to that party on the east side," Monica said.

Michael stomped around a little and rubbed his head. "Isabel, why didn't you tell me this before?"

"When was I supposed to do that? While you were in here doing your set-up?"

"Ten bucks says his parents grounded him," Tommy said.

"But why wouldn't he *call?*" Michael said. "He's the only one who can do sound."

"I might be able to handle it if he doesn't show," Tommy said. "That board isn't much different than what I use with my guitar."

"You can't do sound and operate the camera at the same time," Michael said.

Me, I wanted to tell him; I can operate the camera; you showed me, remember? However, that wasn't why I was there. My role was to scream.

"All right, let's rehearse," Michael said. "Paxton, we'll take it from where you come through the door. I'll worry about Ron later," he said, sounding worried.

What is the *main* challenge facing the characters in this story?

A Will Isabel play her part well?

B Will Michael get his movie made?

C Will Michael recognize Isabel's worth?

D Will Isabel be harmed during the making of the movie?

This question is about how the characters and events interact. You know Isabel wants to do more to help than just playing the victim, and you can predict that events will happen that way. Whatever Isabel does, however, it will be in support of Michael and his movie. The correct answer is choice B.

Which of these sentences *best* describes Michael in this story?

A He thinks that he has to do everything himself.

B He doesn't care much about other people's feelings.

C His attention is totally focused on making his movie.

D He doesn't really know anything about making movies.

Did you notice how Michael changes between the first part of the story and the second? In the first part, he's laughing with his friends. In the second part, he's all business. He knows how to control a movie set. He knows what jobs need to be done, and he assigns people to do them. He teases his sister, but nothing suggests that he's unkind to Isabel or to the other characters. He's been preparing for this film project for some time, though, and right now everything else is channeled through it. Choice C is the correct answer.

What is the role of Tommy's basement in the story?

_____

_____

_____

_____

Can a setting "play a role"? Yes, if it affects the characters and events of the story. You learned in the first part of the story why Michael wanted to film a horror movie there. Isabel's description of the setting and her feelings about it may make you appreciate Michael's choice. Here is a sample answer:

The basement is a gloomy, cramped space, and the characters are going to spend most of the next two days there. Some of them may end up feeling like Isabel does, uncomfortable and a little scared. On the other hand, it may make for a really good scary movie. "On the set," Michael seems transformed from a teen to a movie director.

In the first part of the story, how does the author use flashback?

_____

_____

_____

_____

The story begins with Michael telling Isabel, "We got horror." This doesn't make sense until you learn something about the 48-Hour Film Project (a real event, by the way). Here is a sample answer:

In the first part of the story, there's a section starting at paragraph 4 that describes in flashback Michael's signing up for the project and explaining it to Isabel. The first part continues in flashback, to show the team gathering and how Isabel feels about the project.

How might Isabel affect the events of the story?

_____

 This question ask you to **make a prediction** based on the characters, the events so far, and the setting. There are many ways that you could answer the question. Here's a sample answer:

Isabel might be asked to operate the camera and do a really good job.

Elements of Drama

Authors have been writing **dramatic literature** to be performed by actors on a stage since the ancient Greeks. In recent times, dramas (like Michael's horror movie) have also been written for radio, film, and video performance. Drama has the same elements of characters, events, and setting as any other story. Dramatic writing, however, uses special features that give instructions to directors and actors for making the story come alive.

A **play** is a story that is performed by actors. A play for the stage is usually divided into **acts** and **scenes.** A scene is part of the action that takes place in one setting.

Characters take part in the play's action. A list of the characters is called the **cast.** It usually appears at the beginning of the play.

The **setting** is the time and place where the action happens. Sometimes the setting is described in a brief introduction that gives the background information about the characters and events in the play.

Dialogue is the words that characters speak. In a **script,** or printed version of a play, dialogue directly follows the character's name.

Stage directions advise actors how to move and speak. In a script, the characters' names, dialogue, and stage directions are printed in different styles of type so that readers can easily spot which is which.

Props are objects that are used by the characters on a stage, such as a book or a pen. **Scenery** is the backgrounds and larger objects that create the setting of the play. **Lighting** refers to the types of lights used on stage and how bright they are. The props, scenery, and lighting are usually described in the stage directions.

UNIT 2 ▨▨▨▨▨▨▨▨▨▨▨▨▨▨▨▨▨▨▨▨▨▨▨▨▨▨▨▨▨▨▨▨▨▨▨
Key Ideas and Details

Guided Practice

Read the play. Then answer the questions.

For the Crime of Voting

a play by Jan Kelter

CHARACTERS:

A barber	Mary
Beverly Jones (male)	Daniel Warner
Edwin Marsh	Newsboys
William Hall	Henry Seldon, a lawyer
Susan B. Anthony	E. J. Keeney, a federal marshal
Guelma	William Storrs
Hannah	Judge Ward Hunt

Women, court officials, and courtroom spectators

> What really happened? With a group, research and report on the career of Susan B. Anthony and her arrest for voting in 1872.

ACT 1, Scene 1

A barbershop in Rochester, New York, the morning of November 1, 1872. A window looks out onto a busy street, where a barber pole stands by the door. A sign in the window, reads REGISTER TO VOTE HERE.

The Barber is shaving a customer. Beverly Jones, Edwin Marsh, and William Hall, election officials, are grouped around a desk. Marsh is the youngest of the three.

BARBER: So, you've already forgotten his service in the late war?

JONES: Sir, I stand second to none in my admiration for General Grant as a soldier. I believe he's been a poor excuse for a president, and I intend on Tuesday to vote for Mr. Greeley.

MARSH: You'll be throwing your vote away, Mr. Jones. Greeley hasn't got a chance, either in this state or in the country at large.

JONES: Mr. Marsh, I don't believe any man in our republic throws his vote away. I know as well as you do that my fellow veterans will turn out in droves in their blue suits, and the general will win in a landslide. I served proudly in the 18th New York Regiment—and I'd enlist again if the rebels were ever to raise the stars and bars of treason. However, I hold the ballot to be sacred, and on Election Day, I intend to cast mine for Mr. Greeley.

BARBER: Nice speech, Jones. Tell me, what office are <u>you</u> running for?

There is laughter among the men, except for Hall, who is looking out the window.

HALL: Gentlemen, here comes trouble.

The door opens and four middle-aged women enter the shop: Susan B. Anthony and her sisters, Guelma, Hannah, and Mary. The three registrars move to confront them; Marsh lagging behind the others.

SUSAN: Good morning, sirs. My sisters and I wish to register to vote.

JONES: Miss Anthony, I don't believe I can register your name.

SUSAN: On what grounds?

JONES: Well, ma'am, as you well know, the Constitution of the State of New York gives the right of franchise only to male citizens.

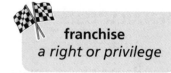
franchise
a right or privilege

SUSAN: Mr. Jones, I assume you are acquainted with the 14th amendment to the <u>United States</u> Constitution?

JONES: I am.

Susan produces a small pamphlet from her handbag and reads from it. The Barber has stopped shaving his customer and is enjoying the spectacle.

SUSAN: "All persons born or naturalized in the United States, and subject to the jurisdiction thereof, are citizens of the United States and of the State wherein they reside. No State shall make or enforce any law which shall abridge the privileges or immunities of citizens of the United States"—<u>All</u> persons, Mr. Jones. Show me where it says anything about male or female.

JONES: Miss Anthony, you know that the 14th amendment was adopted to secure the franchise for the former Negro slaves.

HALL: <u>Male</u> slaves.

SUSAN: I know this, Mr. Jones. If you refuse us our rights as citizens, I will bring charges against you in criminal court, and I will sue each of you personally for large, exemplary damages!

There is a brief pause as the men, stunned, look at each other.

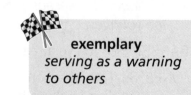
exemplary
serving as a warning to others

MARSH: Miss Anthony, you place us in an awkward position. You're asking us to violate state law.

SUSAN: I am asking you, Edwin—no, <u>demanding</u>—that you honor our rights as citizens of the United States.

JONES: Miss Anthony, this is not our decision to make. This is a question that divides some of the best minds of our country.

HALL *(with relief):* Here's Warner. He'll decide.

Daniel Warner, the registrars' supervisor, enters from the street. When he sees the assemblage he stops short for a moment, sizing up the situation.

WARNER *(warily):* Gentlemen. Ladies.

JONES: Daniel, a word with you?

The men consult. Susan stands with her sisters.

UNIT 2 ▰▰▰▰▰▰▰▰▰▰▰▰▰▰▰▰▰▰▰▰▰▰
Key Ideas and Details

GUELMA: Can they really have us arrested?

SUSAN: <u>They</u> can do what they please. That is precisely the issue. America will never be a free country as long as half its citizens do not have equal rights.

subordinates
people subject to another's orders or supervision

WARNER *(stepping toward them):* Miss Anthony. Ladies. I have instructed my subordinates to allow you to register to vote.

SUSAN *(surprised):* You have?

WARNER *(beckoning them to the registration desk):* Indeed. That will place the onus of the situation squarely on you, won't it?

onus
burden

The women, led by Susan, line up at the desk and begin to sign their names. Lights begin to fade on the scene.

WARNER *(aside):* I'll be hanged if I'll be cowed by that woman!

SUSAN: My name is Susan Brownell Anthony. I live at—

MARSH: I know your address, Ma'am.

The stage is dark. As scenery is being changed for Scene 2, two Newsboys cross the stage in opposite directions hawking newspapers.

NEWSBOY 1: Extra, extra! Susan B. Anthony registers to vote!

NEWSBOY 2: Extra, extra! Forty-seven Rochester women register to vote!

Analyze the play. How does the character of Susan influence the events of the plot?

_____

_____

_____

_____

✔ You know this is a based on an actual incident. However, an author may use **dramatic license** with the facts to make a more interesting story. You need to answer the question based on the play, not on history. Here is a sample answer:

> Susan is driving the action, and the other characters act in response to her. She has put the registrars in a difficult position and encouraged other women to register to vote. She has issued a challenge, and Warner has accepted it. The next move is up to the government.

Determine which of these is an example of scenery used in this play.

A a desk

B a barber

C a handbag

D a newspaper

An object such as a handbag or a newspaper that can be picked up and moved by an actor is a prop. The barber is a character in the play. Scenery is the larger objects that don't get moved around on the stage—such as a desk. Choice A is the correct answer.

Explain how the author uses setting and dialogue to develop the conflict in this play.

_____

_____

_____

_____

_____

_____

The setting is a shop that also functions as a voter-registration office. You already know that the events of the plot are going to center around voting. Here is a sample answer:

The setting is a "male" place—a barbershop, where a man is being shaved, and also an office where only men may be registered to vote. The conflict in the play is an effort to change that situation. The dialogue before Susan enters the shop is about the upcoming election and an American's "sacred" right to vote. Once she's on stage, the dialogue is still about that, but it has become a challenge to the men.

Test Yourself

Odysseus and the Athletes

from The Odyssey, *by Homer, as adapted by James Deare*

At this point in Homer's great epic, the hero Odysseus, exhausted from his encounter with the Cyclops and other adventures, has been shipwrecked in the land of the Phaecians and rescued by Nausicaa, the young daughter of King Alcinous. The gracious king pledges to outfit him with a new ship and calls his lords to a feast to meet the wandering hero.

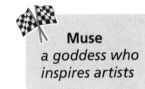

Muse
a goddess who inspires artists

In came the king's bard, whom the Muse adored, and he sang of the fighting heroes who had defeated Troy—Achilles and Agamemnon, and brave Odysseus. None knew it was Odysseus himself who sat before them, clutching his sea-blue cape in his powerful hands, and wiping his eyes with it, ashamed to show his tears. Only Alcinous, sitting beside him, noticed his grief and heard the sighs in his breathing.

"Hear me, my lords!" said the king. "For now we've had enough of feasting and music. Come, let us go out and test ourselves in sports, so that when our guest gets home, he can tell his friends how we Phaecians are unexcelled in the world at boxing, wrestling, jumping, and racing!"

The king led the way along the path from the palace to the meeting grounds. All the people came out to view the games, cheering the athletes: Topsail and Rowhard, Waves-on-the-Shore and Stroke-Oar, Race-the-Wind and Seagirt—and Broadsea, a match for the war-god Ares. Alcinous's sons came too, Laodamas and his brothers Halius and Clytoneus.

The games began. The first event was a footrace on the beach, and Clytoneus the prince was faster than all the rest. Next came the wrestling, and the powerful Broadsea could not be matched. In the jumping, it was Seagirt who beat the field, and the king's son Laodamus boxed all comers to the sand.

When the crowd had at last had enough of games, Laodamus said to the other athletes, "Come, friends, let's ask our guest if he enjoys any sport. Look at him—he's not past his prime, and though he's been beaten down by blows, he has an athlete's build."

Broadsea said, "Well put, Laodamus. Go on, challenge him yourself."

The prince stood up before Odysseus and said, "Come stranger, won't you compete against us, just for fun? You'll soon be leaving us; your ship's already been hauled down to the sea."

"Laodamus," Odysseus said sharply, "why do you mock me with a challenge? I'm too care-laden now for sports. I've suffered and struggled for years, and here I've come begging your people, begging your king, wanting only a ship home."

"I knew it!" said Broadsea, and he grinned in his face. "I figured you for some sort of merchant, not a real man. You're only out for gold. I can see you're no athlete."

With that, Odysseus shot back darkly, "And I can see that you're a fool. The gods don't hand out all their gifts to everyone—not strength and brains and a nimble tongue to all. Look at you—a god could not improve upon your looks, but when you open your mouth you show your mind is worthless. I've grappled with the wars of men and with Poseidon's storms. Nevertheless, I'll give your games a try!"

Up he jumped, despite his heavy cloak, and seized a discus—heavier by far than the ones the Phaecians had used. He wheeled around and let fly with his great hand. The sailors waiting by the ship ducked as it flew by. Great Athena, in her guise as a man, cried out, "Even a blind man could find your mark—it's so far in front of the others! There's none can touch you in this event!"

At this Odysseus laughed, so glad to find a friend in the crowd. "Now match that, you cubs!" he cried to the Phaecian athletes. "All of you, anyone who has the guts—step right up and try me at boxing, wrestling, racing—all except Laodamus, my host. Who could be so worthless as to fight his friend? I'm not half bad at archery either. Only at sprinting would you outdo me, for the sea has taken the spring from my legs."

All stood silent then. Only Alcinous stepped forward to answer. "Stranger," he said, "friend—nothing you've said sounds unseemly. You want to show your skill, stung that a disrespectful young man should ridicule you. But come—when you sit in your own halls someday, your family and your lords by your side, I would that you could tell them of our talents. We're no great fighters, we Phaecians, but we can run like the wind, and none can touch us on the sea. Dearer to us still are feasting, music, and dance. Come, let our dancers put on a show for you, that you may tell your friends how far we excel the world!"

Poseidon
the sea god, who hates Odysseus

Athena
goddess who inspires people with courage

1 What is the conflict in this tale? What is the event that sets the conflict in motion?

_____

_____

_____

_____

_____

2 What event moves the setting of the story outdoors?

   A The king does not want his guest troubled by the bard's songs.

   B The ship and crew the king promised Odysseus is ready to sail.

   C The Phaecians have planned a sports competition as entertainment.

   D The king wants to impress Odysseus with his people's athletic gifts.

3 Which of these *best* explains Alcinous's attitude toward Odysseus?

   A As a king, his duty is to help strangers in his land.

   B He admires Odysseus for his exploits in the Trojan War.

   C He feels obliged to help Odysseus because his daughter rescued him.

   D The Phaecians are a sea-going people, and Odysseus is a brave man of the sea.

4 How does the character of Odysseus determine his two responses to the Phaecians' challenge?

_____

_____

_____

_____

_____

5 How does the sea function as both a setting and as a character in Odysseus's story?

_____

_____

_____

_____

_____

UNIT 2 ▨▨▨▨▨▨▨▨▨▨▨▨▨▨▨▨▨▨▨▨▨▨▨▨▨▨▨▨▨▨
Key Ideas and Details

Analyzing Events and Concepts

RI.7.3

Vocabulary
behemoth
formidable
silicon

Ideas, events, and people do not exist independently. In history, business, the arts, indeed in every area of human life, they are constantly interacting with one another. George Washington and Thomas Jefferson, for instance, might have lived out their lives as Virginia planters had not new ideas of freedom and events in the colonies during the 1770s raised them to prominence. Likewise, our nation's early history might have been quite different if other individuals holding different ideas had emerged to lead it. When you read for information, it's important to note and understand how the text reflects these interactions between individuals, ideas, and events.

Guided Practice

Read the passage. Then answer the questions.

Mrs. Gage and Her Son-In-Law

by Stephanie Fay

Matilda Joslyn Gage was supposedly horrified when, in 1882, her youngest daughter Maud announced her intention to marry a struggling actor and playwright. Maud was studying law at a time when there were very few women lawyers, and Mrs. Gage knew that marriage to this dreamer would squelch her daughter's career. Within minutes, though, the formidable Mrs. Gage was laughing at herself. She had devoted her life to the idea that all people had the right to make up their own minds, and Maud was most certainly her mother's daughter. Matilda gave her blessing to the marriage. Until her death in 1898, she would spend several months every year with Maud's family.

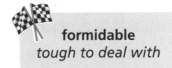

formidable
tough to deal with

Matilda Gage is said to have been "born with a hatred of oppression." As a young woman, she had risked prison by letting her home be a "station" for slaves escaping on the Underground Railroad. A leader of the American women's rights movement, she was considered more radical than others such as Susan B. Anthony, who were chiefly concerned with winning the vote. Gage was active in the struggle for suffrage, but she also championed women's equality under the law, in religion, and especially in family life. She wrote hundreds of articles and published a magazine devoted to women's rights.

Matilda Joslyn Gage

Mrs. Gage got along with her son-in-law, who once called her "the most gifted and educated woman of her age." Lyman Frank Baum had been born into a wealthy family in 1856. He was by no means lazy, but neither was he the practical man his father was. As a boy he liked writing stories. His father bought him a printing press on which he published a neighborhood newspaper. In his teens, he put out a journal on stamp collecting. Later, he tried his hand at raising a fancy breed of chicken, and he published a book on that subject.

The theater was Frank's passion. It was a world of traveling shows, of fantasy and illusion. Baum invested in a theater company that promised him acting roles, and was bilked out of his money. In 1880, his father built him a theater in Richburg, New York, for which Frank wrote and acted in his own plays. However, a fire destroyed the building, along with the props, costumes, and the scripts to nearly all his plays. He and Maud moved to Aberdeen, on the South Dakota prairie, where tornadoes are a frequent danger. Baum opened a store and later edited a newspaper. Both went broke. The family then moved to Chicago, where Frank worked at several jobs. By 1897, he had achieved modest success with a magazine for advertisers on store window displays. He pioneered the use of mannequins, or "dummies," to model clothes and portray scenes of middle-class life.

Baum was a born storyteller. People who knew him in Aberdeen later recalled how children were always stopping him on the streets, begging for a story. Now, he was making up tales to entertain his four young sons and their friends. Some were his prose versions of "Mother Goose" rhymes. Others were original tales drawn from his years in the theater and his experiences on the South Dakota prairie. Baum had long complained that there were no American fairy tales with American characters, an idea that was in his mind as he spun his stories. They were set in a magic land. Scarecrows, which had always fascinated him, figured prominently in these tales. So did a little girl named Dorothy, the name of his brother's daughter who had died in infancy.

Often his children's grandmother would be part of his audience. Finally one day (or so it is said), Matilda Joslyn Gage confronted her son-in-law: "Frank Baum, if you don't write down those stories of yours and try to publish them, you're a fool!"

Frank Baum may have been a dreamer, but he was no fool. Matilda Gage did not live to see the publication of *The Wonderful Wizard of Oz* and its sequels, but perhaps she would have been as proud of their success as she would have been to see American women voting.

Locate some of L. Frank Baum's stories online and read them. You'll find more than just Oz!

Analyze the passage. How did Matilda Gage's ideas influence her daughter's marriage?

_____

_____

 This passage illustrates how individuals, ideas, and events influence one another. Another 19th-century mother might have opposed her daughter's marriage to an actor-playwright. Here is a sample answer:

Matilda Gage had taught her daughter to be independent and to make up her own mind.

How did the events of L. Frank Baum's early life help make him the person he became? Explain why.

_____

_____

_____

_____

 This question asks you to make an inference. What kind of a person _was_ Baum? How can you tell from the sparse details in the article? Here is a sample answer:

Baum was always busy, always trying new things, and he wasn't bothered by failure, or what other people thought of his ideas. If he was interested in chickens, he published a book about them. When his theater burned down, he moved to South Dakota and opened a store. So, the idea of making up stories like no one had ever written before didn't seem foolish to him.

How did the idea of "American fairy tales" influence the stories Baum wrote?

_____

_____

_____

_____

✓ Here the author assumes that her readers are familiar with Baum's "Oz" stories and with popular children's fairy tales. Here is a sample answer:

> The fairy tales Baum and most Americans knew come from Europe. Their characters are kings, princesses, and magical creatures. Baum wrote tales with American characters that began in American places, like Kansas, and whose magic drew on real American things such as tornadoes and scarecrows.

How did Matilda Gage influence Baum's success as a writer?

_____

_____

✓ This is the main point of the passage: how a women's-rights advocate influenced the creation of a series of fantasy tales. Here is a sample answer:

> Matilda prodded Baum to write down and try to publish his stories, which he had made up initially to entertain his own children.

List in chronological order some key experiences in Baum's life and explain specifically how they influenced Baum as a writer.

_____

_____

_____

_____

_____

_____

✓ Here you have to choose from the events in the article and draw conclusions about how they played on a writer's imagination. Here is a sample answer:

1—Baum was always writing and his father encouraged him.

2—He chose a life in the theater, where he saw how fantasy was created on stage and met some interesting characters.

3—He lived in South Dakota, where he experienced life on the prairie.

4—He had a business involved with designing store windows, which is a kind of fantasy.

5—He made up stories for his children.

A Couple of Geeks in a Garage

by Edward Seaton

The first computer I ever saw was an IBM 7094, when I was at college. It filled a room in the computing center the size of a two-car garage. It took special training to operate. If you had a project that required a computer, you brought your data to the experts at the center, reserved space in the queue, and waited several weeks for them to process it.

That was in 1968. I am writing this article on a MacBook Pro laptop computer. It fills a space between my elbow and my shoulder. I carry it with me and work at my convenience. It can do jobs that those technicians in 1968 couldn't even imagine, and it's faster and more powerful than that garage-sized behemoth.

The story of the personal computer began *in* a garage in 1971. That was where a high-school student named Steve Jobs saw a computer that another friend, a college student named Steve Wozniak, was building. Years later, Jobs recalled that Wozniak "was the first person I met who knew more about electronics than I did."

The two Steves were in the right place at the right time. Both had studied electronics at Homestead High School in Cupertino, California, in an area that was being called "Silicon Valley." New businesses that made computers and computer parts were starting up there every year. The first computers had been developed in the 1940s, during World War II. The U.S. Navy was building guns so powerful that they could hit a ship that was over the horizon and couldn't be seen. One early computer was built to calculate a trajectory so that these guns could be aimed. By the 1950s, computers were being used to solve complicated problems and organize data for the government and the largest businesses. They were too expensive for anyone else. The price began to come down after the transistor was developed. These electronic switching devices made it possible to build computers that

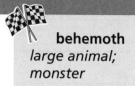

behemoth
large animal; monster

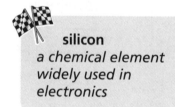

silicon
a chemical element widely used in electronics

ENIAC—First General Purpose Computer

UNIT 2
Key Ideas and Details

were smaller and faster. Then came integrated circuits, fingernail-sized "chips" of silicon that held thousands of transistors. They further increased power and speed and brought the price down to where a university or medium-sized business could afford a computer. One of the inventors of the transistor, William Shockley, started a company near Cupertino. Brilliant young engineers came to work for him, then left to form their own companies. Silicon Valley was born.

That was the situation when the two Steves met. Both Jobs and Wozniak had spent summers working for computer companies. They used what they learned to work on their own hobby projects. By 1975, the two friends were both working full-time in Silicon Valley. Both were excited about an invention called the microprocessor. It made it possible to put all of a computer's "works" on a single chip. Small, fast computers might now be built for a few hundred dollars.

However, who would buy them? The big companies thought that "microcomputers" would be used to control larger computers. The two Steves and their friends at the Homebrew Computer Club, who were building computers from kits, had livelier ideas. "Micros" could be used by small businesses. They could be used for writing, education, and games. They could have hundreds of uses—*if* they could be made "user-friendly" for people who didn't happen to be electronics enthusiasts.

Wozniak set out to build one in his spare time. He wanted to fit all the parts into a small box. He developed a programming language that would let games and other programs be written for his computer.

The popular Apple II, introduced in 1977, had 48,000 bytes of memory. Even a small computer today can store billions of bytes.

Wozniak showed his computer to engineers at the company where he worked. They didn't think much of it. The most interested person was Jobs. He thought they could make a little money by building and selling copies of Wozniak's computer. On April 1, 1976, they started a company. It had the modest goal of making 100 computers. Jobs came up with a name for the company, suggested by a farm where he had once picked apples. By the end of 1980, Apple Computer, Inc. had earned the two Steves "a little money"—between them, nearly $400 million.

Steve Jobs ran the company until shortly before his death in 2011, and Steve Wozniak still contributes ideas. The company is better known today for smart phones and MP3 music players, but I'm still partial to their computers. My MacBook Pro is the seventh Apple I've owned. I still have the first one, an Apple II that I bought in 1978. It still works. I keep it, fittingly, in my garage.

1 Explain how the meeting of the two Steves in a friend's garage influenced future events.

_____

_____

_____

2 According to the article, why were Steve Jobs and Steve Wozniak "in the right place at the right time"?

_____

_____

_____

_____

_____

3 Why, according to the article, did "Silicon Valley" become a center for the computer industry?

_____

_____

_____

_____

_____

4 Explain how a war influenced the development of computers.

_____

_____

_____

_____

_____

5 Analyze the passage. How was the author influenced by the individuals, ideas, and events he describes in the article?

_____

_____

_____

_____

_____

REVIEW

Key Ideas and Details

Vocabulary

betrothed

inclement

Jim Crow laws

precipitating

inclement
rainy, snowy, or stormy weather

Read the story. Then answer the questions.

The Snow Bride

a tale from Japan

There was a woodcutter named Mosaku who had a young apprentice named Minokichi. One winter night, they journeyed to a forest some distance from their village. It was bitterly cold when they neared their destination and saw before them a river. They desired to cross, but the ferryman had gone away, leaving his boat on the other side of the water. As the weather was too inclement to permit swimming across the river, they took shelter in the ferryman's little hut.

Mosaku fell asleep almost as soon as he entered this humble but welcome shelter. Minokichi, however, lay awake for a long time listening to the cry of the wind and the hiss of the snow as it was blown against the door.

Minokichi at last fell asleep, to be soon awakened by a shower of snow falling across his face. He found that the door had been blown open. Standing in the room was a fair-skinned woman in dazzlingly white garments. For a moment she stood thus; then she bent over Mosaku, her breath coming forth like white smoke. After bending thus over the old man for a minute or two, she turned to Minokichi and hovered over him. He tried to cry out, for the breath of this woman was like a freezing blast of wind.

"I had meant to treat you as I have done the old man at your side," she said. "I forbore on account of your youth and beauty. However, you must keep this matter secret. If you dare mention to anyone what you have seen here, you will die instantly."

"I swear it!" said the terrified Minokichi, and at these words, the woman suddenly vanished.

Minokichi called out to his beloved master, "Mosaku, Mosaku, wake! Something very terrible has happened!" However, there was no reply. He touched the hand of his master in the dark, and found it was like a piece of ice. Mosaku was dead.

A year passed. When anyone asked what had happened to old Mosaku, Minokichi only answered, "He froze to death."

One evening the next winter, while Minokichi was returning home from the forest, he chanced to meet a pretty girl by the name of Yuki.[1] She informed him that she was going to Yedo[2], where she desired to find a place as a servant. Minokichi was charmed with this maiden, and he went so far as to ask if she were betrothed. Hearing that she was not, he took her to his own home, and in due time married her.

betrothed
engaged to be married

Yuki presented her husband with ten fine and handsome children, fairer of skin than average. When Minokichi's mother died, her last words were in praise of Yuki, and her eulogy was echoed by many of the country folk in the district.

One night, while Yuki was sewing, the light of a paper lamp shining upon her face, Minokichi recalled the extraordinary experience he had had in the ferryman's hut.

"Yuki," said he, "you remind me so much of a beautiful pale woman I saw when I was 18 years old. She killed my master with her ice-cold breath. I am sure she was some strange spirit, and yet tonight you seem to resemble her."

Yuki flung down her sewing. There was a horrible smile on her face as she bent close to her husband and shrieked, "It was I, Yuki-Onna,[3] who came to you then, and silently killed your master! Oh, faithless wretch, you have broken your promise to keep the matter secret, and if it were not for our sleeping children I would kill you now! Remember, if they have anything to complain of at your hands I shall hear, I shall know, and on a night when the snow falls I will kill you!"

Then Yuki-Onna, the Lady of the Snow, changed into a white mist, and, shrieking and shuddering, passed through the smoke-hole, never to return again.

---

[1]**Yuki:** a popular girls' name in Japan, and also the word for "snow"

[2]**Yedo:** old name for the city of Tokyo

[3]**Yuki-Onna:** "snow woman," a ghost-witch in Japanese folklore

 UNIT 2 ▓▓▓▓▓▓▓▓▓▓▓▓▓▓▓▓▓▓▓▓▓▓▓▓▓▓▓▓▓▓▓▓▓
Key Ideas and Details

1 Determine which of these *best* expresses the theme of the story.

    A   Always keep your promises.

    B   Do not be in a hurry to marry.

    C   Let what is past remain in the past.

    D   Snow can be beautiful, but also deadly.

2 What evidence from the story supports your answer to question 1?

_____

_____

_____

_____

_____

3 Explain why the two men have to spend the night in the hut.

_____

_____

_____

_____

_____

4 What details help you picture the snow-witch?

_____

_____

_____

_____

_____

5 Analyze the passage. In what two ways does the text hint that Yuki is really the snow-witch?

_____

_____

_____

_____

6 Explain how the setting in the opening paragraph shapes the plot of the story.

_____

_____

_____

_____

7 Analyze how the character of Minokichi determines the climax of the plot.

_____

_____

_____

_____

8 Write a summary of the story.

_____

_____

_____

_____

Who's Driving This Bus?

by Peter Binford

What makes history go? What is the driving force behind the events that build or transform nations or the world? Before 1750, most historians would have answered "God," "the gods," or "destiny"—usually as a way of justifying the place in history of their own particular nation, tribe, or religious group. By the middle of the 19th century, the "Great Man" theory had become the usual way of explaining history, maintaining that great events result mainly from the thoughts or actions of exceptional individuals. A more modern idea is that great men or women are simply the product of their time. Their actions would be impossible without social conditions that began before they came on the scene. From my reading of history, it seems that the answer sometimes is "all of the above."

Take for instance the Montgomery, Alabama, bus boycott of 1955–56. The boycott is often cited as the precipitating event of the African American civil-rights struggle, and Rosa Parks and Dr. Martin Luther King Jr. are its certified heroes. However, what if Mrs. Parks hadn't been riding on the bus on that fateful December 1, 1955? What if young Dr. King had become an assistant minister at his father's church in Atlanta and never come to Montgomery at all? Would history have turned out any different?

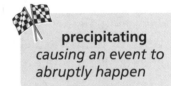

precipitating
causing an event to abruptly happen

Taking a "what if" position with regard to history is an empty argument and thus no argument at all. Let's take a look instead at what actually happened. Rosa Parks, as everyone knows, refused to give up her seat for a white passenger. She was arrested under the Jim Crow laws in force at the time and taken to jail. Word of her arrest spread quickly in the African American community. The next day she was bailed out by E. D. Nixon and Clifford Durr of the Montgomery chapter of the National Association for the Advancement of Colored People (NAACP), for which Parks served as secretary. On Sunday, December 4, plans for a boycott were announced in black churches. The following evening, a meeting was held at the Mount Zion AME Church to discuss strategies. An organization called the Montgomery Improvement Association (MIA) was set up, and Dr. King was chosen to lead it. The rest, as they say, is history.

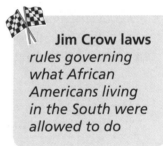

Jim Crow laws
rules governing what African Americans living in the South were allowed to do

Let's take a look at some of "the rest": A movement for equal rights had been building in America before 1955. Though it met with fierce resistance, it did not begin on that bus. "Jim Crow" had been successfully challenged in the streets and in the courts, in U.S. government employment in 1941, and in professional baseball in 1947. The 1954 *Brown v. Board of Education* decision had struck down segregation in public schools.

In Montgomery, E. D. Nixon and other African American community leaders had been planning to challenge the bus segregation laws. In March 1955, a black teen named Claudette Colvin was arrested for refusing to give up her seat to a white man, on the same bus line as Mrs. Parks nine months later. No boycott was organized as a result of her arrest. Because of her personal issues, it was decided that she wouldn't make the best test case.

The boycott that developed over Mrs. Parks' arrest seemed to arise almost spontaneously. E. D. Nixon, on the evening he bailed Parks out of jail, later met with Jo Ann Robinson, a college professor and political leader. That night her group, the Women's Political Council, printed up 35,000 leaflets urging African Americans to boycott the bus system. They were distributed the day of Parks's trial, December 5. That evening Dr. King was installed as leader of the MIA, but the boycott was already in motion. The next day, about 40,000 black commuters stayed off the buses. The boycott lasted 381 days. During that time, Dr. King's home was bombed, and Nixon's was also attacked. The boycott was eventually settled by a court case that had nothing to do with Rosa Parks. By then, she had become an international symbol of the civil-rights struggle, and King had been anointed as its leader.

"No one can understand the action of Mrs. Parks unless he realizes that eventually the cup of endurance runs over, and the human personality cries out, 'I can take it no longer,'" Dr. King wrote. As Rosa Parks remembered many years afterward, "I did not want to be mistreated. I did not want to be deprived of a seat that I had paid for. It was just time."

It was just time. That's something that can be said about any historical movement—taking nothing away from great leaders, or from changes that point toward sweeping change.

9 How does Binford's title reflect the main idea of his article? How does it reflect the example he uses to illustrate this idea?

_____

_____

_____

_____

_____

10 The first paragraph mainly ____.

    A summarizes three competing theories about history

    B states the author's qualifications to write about history

    C expresses skepticism about religious theories of history

    D explains why you can't make generalizations about history

11 The author's second central idea is that ____.

    A There's really no such thing as a "great leader."

    B Asking "What if?" about history doesn't yield answers.

    C Group action, and not individual leaders, are what change history.

    D The bus boycott would have happened without Rosa Parks or Martin Luther King.

12 Analyze how the author develops his central ideas over the course of this article.

_____

_____

_____

_____

_____

13 Explain how the author shows that a challenge to the bus segregation law was being planned before Rosa Parks' arrest.

_____

_____

_____

_____

_____

14 How does the author demonstrate that ideas influence events?

_____

_____

_____

_____

15 How does the author demonstrate that events influence individuals?

_____

_____

_____

_____

16 List in order the events after Rosa Parks's arrest that resulted in the Montgomery bus boycott.

_____

_____

_____

_____

17 Write a summary of the article.

_____

_____

_____

_____

UNIT 2 ▚▚▚▚▚▚▚▚▚▚▚▚▚▚▚▚▚▚▚▚▚▚▚▚▚▚▚▚▚▚▚▚▚
Key Ideas and Details

Craft and Structure

There's more to writing than putting down words and sentences. There's a craft to it, just as there is to building a house. A writer considers the language he uses with respect to his purpose for writing and his audience. The writer puts together verses, sentences, stanzas, paragraphs, and chapters in ways that help move a story, poem, or an article forward or make the information she is presenting clearer. Any writer has a point of view and purpose for writing and will craft his sentences, paragraphs, and longer units to support them.

This unit is about the ways that writers craft and structure their work and their reasons for doing it. As you read, it's important to recognize this craft and structure, just as you can recognize in the work of a carpenter or electrician how they make a house livable and perhaps even beautiful.

- **In Lesson 8,** you'll learn about craft and structure in literary texts: how paragraphs and chapters, stanzas and scenes fit together to form a whole, and how the structure an author chooses contributes to the meaning of the text.

- **Lesson 9** is about craft and structure in informational text. You'll learn about the different ways that writers structure their work to present information, how the structure they choose depends on the kind of information they want you to know, and how different sections fit together to form a whole and to develop the ideas.

- **Lesson 10** is about point of view in literary and informational texts. You'll learn how the point of view of an author, speaker, or narrator influences the way events in a story or poem are narrated, and how different characters or narrators can express different points of view. In reading informational text, you'll learn how to recognize the author's purpose for writing, how that purpose reflects the author's point of view, and how the author distinguishes her point of view from that of others.

Literary Structure

RL.7.4, RL.7.5

Vocabulary
chimney-piece
habeas corpus
mead
preposterous
temperance
wrought

Writers choose different forms to present their ideas. A novel, a short story, and a narrative poem all do the same job, but the story the writer wants to tell will determine which form she chooses. Poems come in dozens of forms, but the form the poet chooses may depend on the nature of the story he wants to tell or the feelings he wants to express. A modern poet may tell a story in free verse that a poet of earlier times might have told in a rhymed ballad. A play tells a story, too, but the author has no narration with which to convey her meaning. It must be done through dialogue and the actor's art. When you read literature, your ideas about the author's meaning are enhanced by understanding why he chose a particular form and structure.

Guided Practice

Read the poem. Then answer the questions.

Offering

by Onitsura

Dry chrysanthemums
Long ago were seventeen—
These, my offering

Which of the following describes the form of this poem?

A haiku

B ballad

C sonnet

D limerick

Lesson 2 briefly described some of the different forms of poetry. This poem is not a narrative poem, a 14-line lyric poem, or a five-line nonsense poem. It is a haiku, a Japanese verse form written in three lines containing five, seven, and five syllables respectively. The correct answer is choice A.

Interpret the double meaning of "seventeen" in the poem.

_____

_____

 An author of haiku has to pack a lot of meaning into three lines. Onitsura, who lived 1660–1738, wrote this one toward the end of his life. Like the flowers that once were vibrantly alive, he thinks of himself as "dried up." Here is a sample answer:

Seventeen is a way of saying that the poet and the chrysanthemums once were young—and it's also the number of syllables in the poem.

Interpret the double meaning of "offering" in the haiku.

_____

_____

 The illustration on page 98 hints at Onitsura's meaning. He wrote this, his last haiku, at age 73 upon becoming a Buddhist priest. Buddhists traditionally honor the Buddha by offering flowers to his image. Here is a sample answer:

The double-meaning of "offering" means an offering of flowers and also an offering of a poem.

Explain how the haiku form contributes to the author's meaning.

_____

_____

 Try explaining the meaning of Onitsura's poem in 17 syllables. Can't do it, can you? That's what makes a haiku special. Here is a sample answer:

The haiku form compresses a lot of images into one brief glance. The poet is reflecting on his old age, comparing himself to the flowers, comparing his poems to the flowers, and saying that for what years remain to him, religion and not poetry will be his life.

On the Grasshopper and Cricket

by John Keats

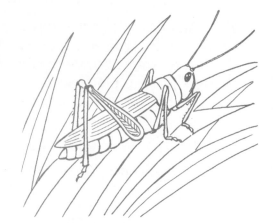

The poetry of earth is never dead:
When all the birds are faint with the hot sun,
And hide in cooling trees, a voice will run
From hedge to hedge about the new-mown mead[1];
5   That is the Grasshopper's—he takes the lead
In summer luxury—he has never done
With his delights; for when tired out with fun
He rests at ease beneath some pleasant weed.
The poetry of earth is ceasing never:
10 On a lone winter evening, when the frost
Has wrought[2] a silence, from the stove there shrills
The Cricket's song, in warmth increasing ever,
And seems to one in drowsiness half lost,
The Grasshopper's among some grassy hills.

Explain what characteristics help you identify this poem as a sonnet.

_____

_____

   English-language poets have been writing sonnets since the 16th century (Keats died in 1821, age just 25), and are still writing them today. You read one by Edgar Allan Poe in Lesson 2. You'll be able to recognize them now when you encounter them. Here is a sample answer:

A sonnet is a lyric poem with 14 lines of ten syllables each and a regular pattern of rhyme.

¹mead: meadow

²wrought: crafted

 UNIT 3
Craft and Structure

If you were to divide this poem into two parts to consider its structure and meaning, you would break it after _____.

A line 4

B line 7

C line 8

D line 10

Another characteristic of a sonnet is the *volta,* an Italian word that means "turn." It summarizes or gives a fresh look to the theme of a poem. In Keats's sonnet, the first eight lines talk about summer and the grasshopper. Line 9 begins a contrasting section about winter and the cricket, which focuses the theme of being indoors on a cold winter day while daydreaming about summer. The correct answer is choice C, and by the way, did you notice that Onitsura's haiku also has a turn?

How does the poet use repetition to convey meaning?

_____

_____

_____

_____

One way that you recognized the "turn" is by the way line 9 *almost* repeats the first line of the poem. With this repetition, Keats introduces something new. Here is a sample answer:

> Keats uses repetition to compare and contrast summer and winter. The first eight lines are full of warm images and summer sounds, while the last six center on "frost" and "silence." But the almost-repeated lines 1 and 9 remind us that both are "the poetry of earth."

Analyze the poem. How does the rhyme pattern change between the two sections of the poem?

_____

_____

_____

✓ Rhymed poems usually follow a rhyme scheme, described by letters of the alphabet. For example, a **rhyme scheme** in which line 1 rhymes with line 3 and line 2 rhymes with line 4 is described as "ABAB." Examine the rhyme scheme of Keats's sonnet and you'll see that it's another way he contrasts the two sections of the poem. Here is a sample answer:

> The first eight lines follow a two-line rhyme scheme, ABBA and CDDC. The last six lines follow a scheme in which the rhymes are divided into three-line groups, EFGEFG.

Contrast how Onitsura's "Offering" and Keats's "On Grasshopper and Cricket" convey their meaning.

_____

_____

_____

_____

✓ Just imagine that Keats had decided to write this poem as a haiku rather than as a sonnet. It might have gone something like this: "Winter's cricket shrills/warm songs from the stove; becomes/summer's grasshopper." You'd miss out on the singing quality of the poem, and also on the rich imagery Keats uses to describe the seasons. Likewise, think of how Onitsura's theme might have sounded mawkish and self-pitying if he had written a sonnet! Here is a sample answer:

> A haiku is a more disciplined form of poem. The poet expresses a single image or two contrasting images in a brief space and leaves it to the reader to expand on the images in her mind to create meaning. A sonnet explores a theme in rich detail with lots of imagery. One is like a photograph, the other like a movie.

UNIT 3 ▨▨
Craft and Structure

Review the scene from "For the Crime of Voting" on pages 73–75 before reading the next passage, from later in the play. Use what you learn from *both* parts of the play to answer the questions.

For the Crime of Voting (continued)

by Jan Kelter

ACT 1, Scene 2

The law office of Henry Selden. Selden sits behind a desk, with Susan B. Anthony in a chair opposite him.

SELDEN: You are determined to go through with this?

SUSAN: I am, Mr. Selden.

SELDEN: You know that you will likely be arrested by federal marshals if you vote tomorrow?

SUSAN: I am counting on it, sir. I want my arrest to be as public as possible. I expect you as my attorney to file a writ of habeas corpus on the grounds that it is no crime for a citizen of the United States to vote.

SELDEN *(sighs):* Miss Anthony. As your attorney, and as a former judge, I agree with your reading of the 14th Amendment. I have advised you that the only way to find out what the law is upon a subject is to bring a test case. However, as one who respects and admires you… Miss Anthony, are you prepared to be taken away in handcuffs? To be hauled off to jail? Do you know what low sort of women with whom you will find yourself incarcerated?

SUSAN: Women like myself, who perhaps have not had my social advantages but who share with me and with every citizen the right to vote. *(a pause)* Mr. Selden, I believe you knew my father. *(Selden nods.)* He and my mother raised my sisters and me to believe firmly in equal rights for all people. It was a loss of innocence when I learned that the majority does not feel this way. If a woman is unmarried, law and custom do not permit her the education and employment required to earn a substantial living. If she marries, the law requires her to yield her property to her husband. If he is a poor man, she is treated henceforth as a slave. If he is a rich man, at best she can expect to be treated as a doll.

She gets up from her chair, agitated, but quickly composes herself. During the rest of her monologue, Selden makes occasional gestures as if to interrupt her, but she will not be interrupted.

SUSAN: At best, Mr. Selden, if he is a kind and sober man. No, do not ask for my silence, please. I have been silenced in temperance meetings and in abolition meetings, and all on account of my sex.

habeas corpus
literally, "you have a body"—a legal process by which a judge determines whether the government may keep someone in jail

temperance
a 19th-century movement against the sale and use of alcoholic drink

You may not know how many women are regularly beaten by their husbands. You may not know it, because they would have no recourse to legal counsel, assuming they could afford it, and therefore no reason to seek it. You must not assume that only poor men beat their wives. It happens in the most respectable homes. In this as in other matters, the female has no rights. Under the law, she is her husband's property. Under the law, to obtain a divorce she must abase herself to the extent that respectable society regards her as no better than those unfortunate women to whom you are so reluctant to place me next to in our county jail. And why, Judge Selden? Because we are constrained from exercising the fundamental right to participate in the process that makes the laws—the very right that defines citizenship in a free country. Do I make myself plain?

SELDEN: Quite plain, Miss Anthony.

SUSAN: So no, I am not afraid of jail. If my being jailed for the crime of voting can bring this nation one step closer to realizing how unjust this custom is that keeps half of us unfree—how preposterous it is—well then, I welcome those handcuffs.

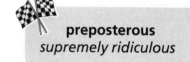

preposterous
supremely ridiculous

SELDEN *(troubled):* Well, then, I may see you in jail.

SUSAN: Perhaps, Mr. Selden. But you *will* see me tomorrow at the polls.

Why did the author choose to have Susan deliver a monologue in this scene? How does this form contribute to its meaning in the play?

_____

_____

_____

_____

 A **monologue** is a "solo" speech in a play delivered to other characters as well as to the audience. (Compare it with a **soliloquy,** which a character delivers to an empty stage, to reveal her thoughts to the audience but not to other characters.) Here is a sample answer:

The monologue lets you understand Susan's life story, how she formed her beliefs and convictions about women's rights, and why she's prepared to go to jail. Since this is a play, the only way to convey this information in a natural way is by having her speak it.

UNIT 3
Craft and Structure

How might this information have been presented differently in a historical novel or a biography?

_____

_____

_____

In a play, dialogue is the only way an author can use words to convey information. In a book, the author has other ways of doing it. Here is a sample answer:

> In a novel, you could show some experiences that formed Susan's beliefs, like being silenced in the temperance and abolition meetings, and the author could tell you what she is thinking without having her speak the words. A biography could do the same thing in a factual way and could also quote from her speeches.

Analyze the play. How does the author's use of language emphasize the setting of the play?

_____

_____

_____

We don't know how people actually spoke in the 19th century. All we can go by is the way people wrote. One characteristic you notice from reading 19th-century authors is that educated people were much more formal in their choice of words and the way they put sentences together than we are today. The dialogue in Kelter's play reflects this. Here is a sample answer:

> The characters speak formally. They address each other as "Mr." and "Miss." They don't use slang or bad grammar. Their sentence construction isn't the way people speak or write today.

Examine how the repetition of phrases and sounds in Susan's monologue affects your reading of the scene.

_____

_____

_____

_____

 Repetition gives a kind of rhythm to speech. It's an aspect of **rhetoric,** or the way people express themselves in writing and speaking. Here is a sample answer:

Several times, Susan begins a series of sentences with the same or similar words and phrases. "If…" "You may not know…" "You must not assume…" "Under the law…" This gives a kind of beat and excitement to her speech, like in a rap song.

Test Yourself

The Mad Gardener's Song

by Lewis Carroll

He thought he saw an elephant
That practiced on a fife:
He looked again, and found it was
A letter from his wife.
5 "At length I realize," he said,
"The bitterness of life!"

He thought he saw a buffalo
Upon the chimney-piece[1]:
He looked again, and found it was
10 His sister's husband's niece.
"Unless you leave this house," he said,
"I'll send for the police!"

He thought he saw a rattlesnake
That questioned him in Greek:
15 He looked again, and found it was
The middle of next week.
"The one thing I regret," he said,
"Is that it cannot speak!"

He thought he saw a banker's clerk
20 Descending from the bus:
He looked again, and found it was
A hippopotamus.
"If this should stay to dine," he said,
"There won't be much for us!"

25 He thought he saw a kangaroo
That worked a coffee mill:
He looked again, and found it was
A vegetable-pill.
"Were I to swallow this," he said,
30 "I should be very ill!"

He thought he saw a coach-and-four
That stood beside his bed:
He looked again, and found it was
A bear without a head.
35 "Poor thing," he said, "poor silly thing!
It's waiting to be fed!"

---

[1]**chimney-piece:** the mantelpiece of a fireplace

He thought he saw an albatross
That fluttered round the lamp:
He looked again, and found it was
40 A penny postage stamp.
"You'd best be getting home," he said:
"The nights are very damp!"

He thought he saw a garden-door
That opened with a key:
45 He looked again, and found it was
A double rule of three:
"And all its mystery," he said,
"Is clear as day to me!"

He thought he saw an argument
50 That proved he was the pope:
He looked again, and found it was
A bar of mottled soap.
"A fact so dread," he faintly said,
"Extinguishes all hope!"

> The rule of three is an idea in English writing that things grouped in threes are funnier or more effective than other numbers.

A Clerihew

by Aurelius Rockslide

Lewis Carroll
Dressed in gentlemen's apparel.
He viewed the world with malice
For believing he had only written "Alice."

> A clerihew is a four-line "biographical" nonsense poem, invented by Edmund Clerihew Bentley.

1 Compare these two poems. What do they *most* have in common?

_____

_____

_____

_____

_____

2 How does the form of "The Mad Gardener's Song" contribute to its meaning?

_____

_____

_____

_____

_____

3 Choose any stanza of "The Mad Gardener's Song." How does the author's use of rhymes and rhythms affect the feeling and sense of the stanza?

_____

_____

_____

_____

_____

4 Explain the several jokes in stanza 3 of "The Mad Gardener's Song" by referring to the stanza's structure.

_____

_____

_____

_____

_____

5 Analyze "A Clerihew." How does the poem's form reflect its meaning?

_____

_____

_____

_____

_____

6 Examine how the rhymes and rhythms of "A Clerihew" affects your reading of the poem.

_____

_____

_____

_____

_____

UNIT 3 ▨▨▨▨▨▨▨▨▨▨▨▨▨▨▨▨▨▨▨▨▨▨▨▨▨▨▨▨▨▨▨▨▨▨▨▨▨▨
Craft and Structure

Text Features

RI.7.5, RH.7.5, RST.7.5

Vocabulary

caravel, dhow
cytoplasm
enigmatic
exotic
organelles

Just as a story, poem, or play is structured as a series of chapters, stanzas, or scenes, informational text is also carefully structured by its author, the better to organize the information and present the ideas. There are many ways that a text may be structured.

Sequence and Chronological Order

One way authors organize information is by presenting it as a series of events or steps. When you read, you need to be able to understand the correct **sequence** in which events or steps happen. Whether you are reading about historical events, a procedure in a science experiment, or instructions for assembling something from a kit, you need to follow the sequence.

| You plan your writing. | → | You write a draft. | → | You revise your draft. | → | You edit your details. | → | You publish your writing. |

A chronological text is not always written in sequential order. For example, a book about a presidential election campaign may begin with the inauguration and then "flash back" to the candidate's early career and decision to run. You can follow the sequence by looking for clues. Watch for words that indicate time, such as *1960, March 14, the next autumn,* and *11:00 p.m.* Look for other words that indicate sequence, too.

Cause and Effect

Another way that authors organize information is by showing connections between ideas and events that explain why things happen. Your reading makes more sense when you understand these *why* connections. Look for clue words that signal **cause and effect.** The thing that happens is the **effect.** Words such as *then, so, led to, as a result, in order that,* and *therefore* signal an effect. The reason why it happens, or what made it happen, is the **cause.** Words like *because, since, reason for, due to,* and *on account of* signal causes.

Comparison and Contrast

A third way writers organize information is by pointing out similarities and differences. When you note similarities between two things, actions, or ideas, you're comparing. When you note differences between them, you're contrasting.

This Venn diagram compares and contrasts two New World empires of the 15th century.

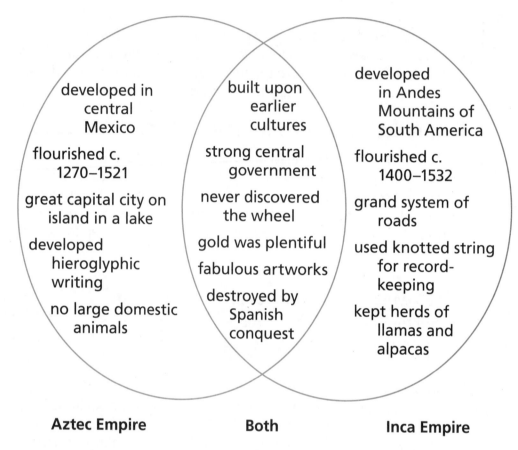

Aztec Empire	Both	Inca Empire
developed in central Mexico	built upon earlier cultures	developed in Andes Mountains of South America
flourished c. 1270–1521	strong central government	flourished c. 1400–1532
great capital city on island in a lake	never discovered the wheel	grand system of roads
developed hieroglyphic writing	gold was plentiful	used knotted string for record-keeping
no large domestic animals	fabulous artworks	kept herds of llamas and alpacas
	destroyed by Spanish conquest	

The middle of the diagram shows how the Aztec and Inca cultures were similar. It **compares** the two empires. The outer part of each circle shows how the two were different. They **contrast** the two empires.

These are some other ways that authors might choose to organize information:

- as a series of problems and solutions (for example, a guide for diagnosing and fixing problems with a phone)

- as a series of questions and answers (for example, an interview)

- in order of importance, from greatest to least (for example, a news story)

Can you think of others?

Guided Practice

Taco Salad

Ingredients:

1 red bell pepper

1 cup plain low-fat yogurt

1 teaspoon hot sauce

3 small tomatoes

4 cups shredded greens (romaine, red-leaf, and butter lettuce)

1 15-oz. can black beans

1 4-oz. can black olives

1 14-oz. can corn

tortilla-shell bowls

1 cup shredded cheddar cheese

salt and pepper to taste

Directions:

1. Using tongs, carefully place the bell pepper under the broiler. Broil, turning occasionally, until the pepper is almost completely black on the outside.

2. Place the blackened pepper in a small bowl and cover tightly with plastic wrap. Let stand ten minutes. Peel the skin off and cut the pepper in half. Discard the seeds.

3. Place the roasted pepper, yogurt, and hot sauce in a blender and purée till smooth. Season with salt and pepper.

4. Cut the tomatoes in half and remove the seeds. Dice into bite-sized pieces and set aside.

5. Drain the canned beans, olives, and corn, and place in a large bowl with the salad greens. Pour the pepper mix in the bowl and toss until well mixed.

6. Divide the salad among the tortilla bowls and sprinkle with shredded cheese. Place some of the chopped tomatoes on top of each salad and top with a spoonful of yogurt. Serves 4.

Which of these *best* describes how the passage is organized?

A   It describes a step-by-step process.

B   It describes a series of causes and effects.

C   It defines a problem and then explains the solution.

D   It presents information in order of importance, from greatest to least.

A recipe is a familiar example of one way that information can be organized. It typically is arranged in two sections, like this one, for ease of use and convenience. However, the ingredients and their amounts could also be mentioned in the second part, as part of the steps where each is used. The key information here is the step-by-step procedure. Choice A is the correct answer.

Explain how the first section contributes to the usefulness of the passage.

_____

_____

A recipe, like a bus schedule or the instructions that come with a household appliance, is an example of a **functional passage.** You read it for information on how to do a particular task—in this case, make a taco salad. Each major section has its purpose. Here is a sample answer:

The first section lists everything you need, and in the right quantities, so that you can make sure you have everything you need and get it ready before you start.

Determine the specific purpose of steps 1–3 and of steps 4–6.

_____

_____

A closer look at the step-by-step instructions shows you that the main idea—making a taco salad—breaks down into two supporting ideas. Here is a sample answer:

Steps 1–3 tell you how to make the dressing, and steps 4–6 tell you how to make the salad.

UNIT 3 ▨▨▨▨▨▨▨▨▨▨▨▨▨▨▨▨▨▨▨▨▨▨▨▨▨▨▨▨▨▨▨▨▨▨▨▨▨▨▨
Craft and Structure

How To Tell Yourself Apart From a Plant

by Shannon Olsen

Biologists estimate that plants and animals diverged from each other about 1.3 billion years ago. A few hundred million years before then, the "twigs" that were to grow into the main branches of life on Earth are hard to tell apart. However, when plants split off from the branch that would lead to animals (and fungi, and several other large groups of living things), they left the rest of life behind. If some catastrophe were to wipe out all the animals (or the fungi, for that matter), plants would still be here. However, if plants were suddenly to vanish, all other higher forms of life would quickly become extinct. The reason, of course, is that animals (and fungi) ultimately depend on plants for their nourishment, while plants make their own nourishment out of light. The difference, as with nearly everything about life on our planet, is in the cells.

Look at plant and animal cells under a microscope, and you will spot some differences. One major distinction is their shape. Animal cells are more or less round in three dimensions, in the same sense that a balloon filled with water is round. Plant cells form a rectangular pattern, as regular as bricks in a wall. That's because animal cells have only a membrane around them, while plant cells have both a membrane and a semirigid cell wall. An animal cell has one or more small vacuoles that store water, minerals, and waste products. A plant cell has one big vacuole, which stores water and helps maintain the shape of the cell. Both kinds of cell have a nucleus, which contains the DNA. In both types, cytoplasm fills the space between the nucleus and the cell membrane. Looking at the cytoplasm through a very powerful microscope, you'll see that both plant and animal cells contain many organelles—ribosomes, which are the cell's protein factories; mitochondria for producing energy, and other structures for transporting proteins, producing cell movement, and assisting in cell division. One type of organelle that you'll find only in plant cells, however, are the green structures called chloroplasts. It's these guys that create that most basic difference in function between you and a blade of grass or an oak tree.

Use the information in the article and the illustrations to make a Venn diagram comparing and contrasting plant and animal cells.

cytoplasm
the gel-like mass in a cell between the nucleus and the membrane

organelles
small structures within the cytoplasm that do specific jobs in a cell

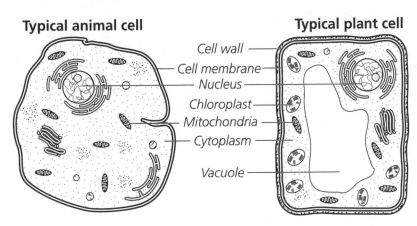

Typical animal cell   **Typical plant cell**

Cell wall
Cell membrane
Nucleus
Chloroplast
Mitochondria
Cytoplasm
Vacuole

Like mitochondria, chloroplasts probably evolved independently as bacteria before being incorporated into more complicated cells a very long time ago. Chloroplasts capture energy from sunlight. Plant cells use this energy to produce nutrients, by the chemical process called photosynthesis. While animals get their food by eating plants, you could say that plants get theirs by eating photons—the enigmatic particles that are the smallest units of light.

enigmatic
puzzling; mysterious

This basic function of plant cells explains a lot about why plants act the way they do. A plant does not need to move to survive, as nearly all animals do, but it does have to grab all the photons it can. That's why plants with leaves dominate most environments. One scientist has compared leaves to solar panels. Natural selection has made them as flat as possible to get the most photons for the least amount of energy. This explains why grasses spread out sideways and why trees compete for photons by growing taller.

One thing about plants that their cells do not explain is why they don't move. It follows that natural selection would have produced at least some plants that could move around for maximum exposure to photons. On the other hand, nature has produced one large group of plants that get animals to do the moving for them. Think about that the next time you see a bee flying from flower to flower.

Analyze the passage. What pattern of organization does it *mainly* follow?

A causes and effects

B order of importance

C chronological sequence

D comparison and contrast

The title helps you focus your reading by telling you, in a humorous way, that this article will be about differences between animals and plants. By the end of the first paragraph, you know that the main idea of the article has to do with cells, and that the differences between plants and animals have to do with their cells. Therefore, the question the passage answers is a *why* question. Notice how often the word *why* and other words that signal cause and effect appear in the passage. The passage may begin with events that happened "a very long time ago," but it doesn't present information chronologically, or in order of importance. It does compare and contrast plant and animal cells, but only as a way of explaining these basic *why* questions. The correct answer is choice A.

How does paragraph 2 contribute to the development of the ideas in the article?

_____

Paragraph 2 is accompanied by the illustration that follows. Its main point is that plant cells contain chloroplasts. The rest of the paragraph supports this idea. Here is a sample answer:

Paragraph 2 compares and contrasts plant and animal cells.

Explain how paragraph 4 contributes to your understanding of the topic.

_____

The main idea of the article is about the characteristics of plant cells and why they are important. Paragraph 4 supports this idea. Here is a sample answer:

Paragraph 4 explains why having chloroplasts results in the way different kinds of plants grow.

According to the article, the main function of chloroplasts in plant cells is _____.

   A to capture photons

   B to expose plants to light

   C to help maintain the structure of the cells

   D to produce nutrients through photosynthesis

This question asks you to use the basic cause-and-effect structure of the article to find specific information. Paragraph 3 talks about chloroplasts and what they do. It explains that photosynthesis happens _as a result_ of the job the chloroplasts do, but that job is something different. The previous paragraph tells you that maintaining the structure of plant cells is the job of the cell walls and vacuoles, while the following paragraph explains why, _because_ of the function of chloroplasts, plants have evolved for maximum exposure to light. That function is "to capture photons." Choice A is the correct answer.

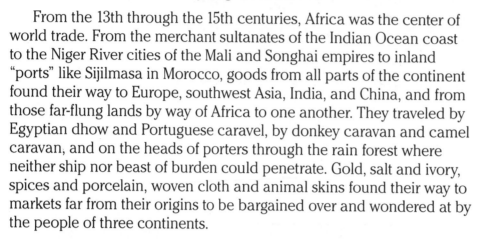

dhow, caravel
types of ships

The Web of Trade

by Eugene Alabi

From the 13th through the 15th centuries, Africa was the center of world trade. From the merchant sultanates of the Indian Ocean coast to the Niger River cities of the Mali and Songhai empires to inland "ports" like Sijilmasa in Morocco, goods from all parts of the continent found their way to Europe, southwest Asia, India, and China, and from those far-flung lands by way of Africa to one another. They traveled by Egyptian dhow and Portuguese caravel, by donkey caravan and camel caravan, and on the heads of porters through the rain forest where neither ship nor beast of burden could penetrate. Gold, salt and ivory, spices and porcelain, woven cloth and animal skins found their way to markets far from their origins to be bargained over and wondered at by the people of three continents.

The key to this trade was Europe's demand for gold. It was one commodity accepted in exchange for goods everywhere. Europe had exhausted most of its own supply of gold, but the rich mines of West Africa had been long known in legend. No doubt these legends were embroidered, and no one in Europe knew exactly where the gold came from, but the mines were real. One gold region, in what is now Guinea, had been the source of wealth for the famous empire of Ghana. A newer and even richer one was located in the forests of the modern nation of the same name.

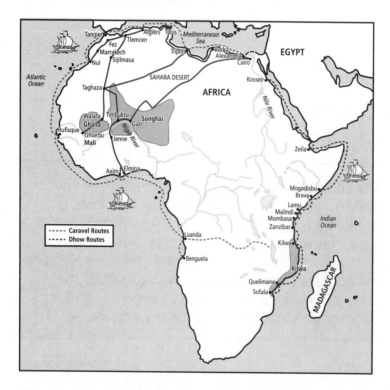

UNIT 3
Craft and Structure

"In the sands of that country is gold beyond telling," wrote a Spanish traveler. "Merchants trade with salt for it, taking the salt on camels.... They start from a town called Sijilmasa and cross the [Sahara] Desert as if it were the sea, [guided by] the stars or rocks.... When they reach [the gold country], they weigh their salt and sell it against a certain weight of gold according to the market and the supply." The gold was carried back across the desert. Other traders brought it by donkey to the Mediterranean coast, where it was exchanged for cloth and metal goods unavailable in Africa. As for the salt, it was carried farther south in great cylindrical blocks into the equatorial regions of Africa where it was sometimes literally worth its weight in gold. There it was exchanged for ivory, kola nuts, and other forest products.

Cities like Timbuktu and Gao, at the southern edge of the Sahara, grew fabulously wealthy on the trade. Another traveler, Leo Africanus, described Gao in the 15th century as "a very large city, about [650 kilometers from] Timbuktu.... Its people are rich merchants who travel constantly about the region with their wares. A great many Blacks come to the city bringing...gold with which to purchase goods imported from [northern Africa] and from Europe, but they never find enough goods on which to spend all their gold and always take half or two-thirds of it home."

Some of the gold made its way eastward across Africa to the Indian Ocean. There a series of ports traded goods with southern and eastern Asia. By far the largest and richest of these ports were Kilwa, in today's Tanzania, and Lamu, in Kenya. Ivory and leopard skins also made their way there across central Africa. They were shipped northward along the coast to Egypt and from there into the Arab lands and Europe. Larger ships awaited the seasonal winds that would carry them to India, Indonesia, and China. They would return laden with silk, spices, and the fine porcelain known to this day as "china." Other traders would bring some of these goods on the long journey to the Mediterranean and to Europe.

Two incidents from the time of this vast trade network stand out. In 1414, a ship from the East African kingdom of Malindi reached China. Among its wares was a live giraffe that somehow had survived the voyage. The exotic animal so impressed the Chinese emperor that he had one of his great fleets escort the Africans home. About the same time, an adventurous Frenchman traveled to the gold country and brought back an African princess as a wife. She came with a train of servants, one of whom became a doctor to the king of France.

exotic
foreign; fascinating because unusual

1 Determine which of these *best* describes how the information in the passage is organized.

   A in chronological sequence

   B as a series of causes and effects

   C from the general to the specific

   D in order of importance, from greatest to least

2 Analyze the passage. How does paragraph 2 develop the main idea of paragraph 1?

_____

_____

_____

_____

3 Analyze how paragraphs 3 through 5 expand on the topic introduced in paragraph 1.

_____

_____

_____

_____

_____

4 The quote from the Spanish traveler in paragraph 3 *mainly* explains the West African gold and salt trade _____.

   A as a step-by-step process

   B as a cause-and-effect relationship

   C as a series of problems and solutions

   D by comparing and contrasting trade routes

UNIT 3
Craft and Structure

5 The quote from Leo Africanus in paragraph 4 *mainly* serves to emphasize ____.

    A how large Gao was in his day

    B how plentiful gold was in West Africa

    C that Africa was a center for world trade

    D that Gao had surpassed Timbuktu in wealth

6 How does the last paragraph illustrate the most important ideas in the article?

_____

_____

_____

_____

_____

Point of View and Author's Purpose

RL.7.6, RI.7.6, RH.7.6

Vocabulary

cerebral

dolefully

epithet

hiatus

straw man

subservient

Anything you read has a point of view. Suppose you're reading about the Black Death, the terrible epidemic that may have wiped out as many as one-third of the population of Europe and western Asia in the years 1347–1350. One author may be writing simply to give you facts and details about history. Another may want to tell an exciting story. Yet another may want to explain the science behind the epidemic. Someone else might be trying to warn her readers against future epidemics. And suppose you read something actually written by a survivor of the Black Death. How does his point of view reflect his time, culture, and social position? Whatever you read, it's important to recognize that the author's point of view and purpose for writing influences the way events are described and topics are explained.

Point of View in Informational Text

In informational text, the author's point of view reflects his purpose for writing. Articles full of facts and details are usually meant to **explain** or **inform.** A passage that contains detailed procedural directions is usually meant to **instruct.** Passages with lots of details that appeal to the senses are probably meant to **describe.** Advertisements, or articles with many opinions, are usually meant to **persuade** the reader to do or believe something.

Guided Practice

Read the passage. Then answer the questions.

Our school's new policy against cell phones in the classroom is unfair, unsafe, and needs to be changed. Cell phones are not a form of entertainment like MP3 players or hand-held game machines. They are a link to our parents in case of emergency, when the school's phone lines would be tied up or out of order. Banning them is comparable to a school of 100 years ago saying that parents couldn't drive their kids to school in cars, only in horse-drawn wagons. It ignores the reality of the way people live today. Yes, phoning or texting during class is distracting, and some students might use their phones to cheat on tests. However, the school's policy doesn't say "Keep your cell phones turned off or in your backpacks." It says "No cell phones." We seventh graders urge Principal Mathur to reconsider her decision.

UNIT 3 ▓▓▓▓▓▓▓▓▓▓▓▓▓▓▓▓▓▓▓▓▓▓▓▓▓▓▓▓▓▓▓▓▓▓
Craft and Structure

What was the author's purpose in writing this passage?

_____

_____

 You probably recognized this passage as an opinion piece, like a newspaper editorial, letter to the editor, or blog post. The author is stating an opinion against her school's policy on cell phones in class, and is trying to persuade someone to agree with her. Here is a sample answer:

> The author's purpose is to persuade the principal to change the school's policy about cell phones.

Which of these sentences *best* states the author's point of view?

A   Cell phones are a necessity in today's world.

B   The school's phone lines are hopelessly out of date.

C   The new policy is an infringement of students' rights.

D   Cell phones are how students communicate with one another.

 In the previous question, about the author's purpose, you identified *what* the author was trying to do. Her point of view is more a matter of *why*: Why does she think the policy needs to be changed? Her stated reason is that cell phones are students' emergency lifelines to their parents. Beyond that is an implied point of view: In our time, cell phones are how people communicate, and not just students with one another. It isn't a matter of rights or a comment on the school's communication system. Her point of view is that a cell-phone ban imposes a hardship on students today. The correct answer is choice A.

Determine how the author distinguishes her point of view from others.

_____

_____

_____

_____

✓ In stating her point of view, the author is implying a contrast with the school principal's point of view. You can infer what Principal Mathur's reasons were for banning cell phones in class. Here is a sample answer:

The author is distinguishing her point of view from the principal's by acknowledging the reasons for the ban—distraction and the possibility of cheating—and pointing out that they are not a problem if the phones are turned off and put away.

How does the author's reference to schools of a hundred years ago advance her point of view?

_____

_____

_____

✓ To determine an author's point of view, you sometimes have to look beyond the literal meaning of her words. "Loaded language" and emphasizing certain facts while avoiding others are tools that authors frequently use to advance their point of view and purpose. Suppose there _has_ been a problem with students using cell phones to cheat, but the author is failing to acknowledge it? Here is a sample answer:

The author implies that the principal is hopelessly out of date by comparing her policy to one supporting the use of horses and wagons in an age of cars.

UNIT 3 ▓▓
Craft and Structure

Point of View in Literary Text

In literary texts, point of view may mean either of two things. First, consider the author's purpose. In any story, the author wants to entertain you, but he may have another purpose. Think about some of your favorite novels. What does the author want you to think about besides the plot? Consider, too, your own point of view. What is the author trying to get you to see and understand? How does he go about doing it?

Point of view in literary text has the second meaning of who is telling the story. In some stories, a character is the narrator. This is called the **first-person point of view.** You can recognize a story told in the first person because the narrator uses the pronouns *I* and *we.*

Other stories are told from a **third-person point of view.** The narrator uses pronouns like *he, she,* and *they* to indicate all the characters. A third-person narrative may take the point of view of one character **(third-person limited).** It may reveal the thoughts of several characters **(third-person omniscient).** Or, it may be told from the point of view of an observer outside the story **(third-person objective).**

Much more rarely, a narrative is told from a **second-person point of view.** The author directly addresses the reader as "you."

Guided Practice

Read the passage. Then answer the questions.

from **Uncle Tom's Cabin**

by Harriet Beecher Stowe

Uncle Tom's Cabin *has been called the most influential novel in American history. It was published in 1852, after the passage of the Fugitive Slave Law made it a federal crime for anyone to help a slave escape. The book was a best seller and added to the conflict between North and South. In this excerpt from Chapter 8, Haley, a dealer in slaves, has bought a black child, Harry, intending to sell him, but Harry's mother, Eliza, has escaped with him to the North. Haley has employed two professional "slave catchers," Loker and Marks, to pursue her. The scene is a tavern in Kentucky.*

"This yer young-un business makes lots of trouble in the trade," said Haley, dolefully.

"If we could get a breed of gals that didn't care, now, for their young uns," said Marks; "tell ye, I think 'twould be bout the greatest mod'rn improvement I know on."

"Jes so," said Haley; "I never couldn't see into it; young uns is heaps of trouble to 'em; one would think, now, they'd be glad to get clar on 'em; but they arn't. And the more trouble a young un is, and the more good for nothing, as a gen'l thing, the tighter they sticks to 'em."

According to an often-told story, when Harriet Beecher Stowe met Abraham Lincoln ten years after the publication of *Uncle Tom's Cabin,* he said, "So you're the little lady who started this great war!"

dolefully
sorrowfully

"Wal, Mr. Haley," said Marks, "Yes, sir, you say 'est what I feel and all'us have.

Now, I bought a gal once, when I was in the trade…and she had a young un that was mis'able sickly; and I jest gin 't away to a man that thought he'd take his chance raising on 't, being it didn't cost nothin'—never thought, yer know, of the gal's taking' on about it—but, Lord, yer oughter seen how she went on. Why, re'lly, she did seem to me to valley the child more 'cause *'t was sickly* and cross, and plagued her; and she warn't making b'lieve, neither—cried about it, she did, and lopped round, as if she'd lost every friend she had. It re'lly was droll to think on 't. Lord, there ain't no end to women's notions."

"Wal, jest so with me," said Haley. "Last summer, I got a gal traded off on me, with a likely lookin' child enough; but, come to look, I found him stone blind. Wal, ye see, I thought there warn't no harm in my jest passing him along, and not sayin' nothin'; and I'd got him nicely swapped off for a keg o' whiskey; but come to get him away from the gal, she was jest like a tiger. So 't was before we started, and I hadn't got my gang chained up; so what should she do but ups on a cotton-bale, like a cat, ketches a knife from one of the deck hands, and, I tell ye, she made all fly for a minit, till she saw 't wan't no use; and she jest turns round, and pitches head first, young un and all, into the river—went down plump, and never ris."

"Bah!" said Tom Loker, who had listened to these stories with ill-repressed disgust, "shif'less, both on ye! *My* gals don't cut up no such shines, I tell ye!"

"Indeed! How do you help it?" said Marks, briskly.

"Help it? Why, I buys a gal, and if she's got a young un to be sold, I jest walks up and puts my fist to her face, and says, 'Look here, now, if you give me one word out of your head, I'll smash yer face in. I won't hear one word.' I says to 'em, 'This yer young un's mine, and not yourn, and you've no kind o' business with it. I'm going to sell it, first chance; mind, you don't cut up none o' yer shines about it, or I'll make ye wish ye'd never been born.' I tell ye, they sees it an't no play, when I gets hold. If one on 'em begins and gives a yelp, why—" and Mr. Loker brought down his fist with a thump that fully explained the hiatus.

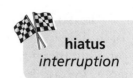

hiatus
interruption

"That ar's what ye may call *emphasis,*" said Marks, poking Haley in the side. "An't Tom peculiar? he! he! I say, Tom, I s'pect…they don't never have no doubt o' your meaning, Tom. If you an't the devil, Tom, you 's his twin brother, I'll say that for ye!"…

"I s'pose you've got good dogs," said Haley.

"First rate," said Marks. "But what's the use? you han't got nothin' o' hers to smell on."

"Yes, I have," said Haley, triumphantly. "Here's her shawl she left on the bed in her hurry; she left her bonnet, too."

"That ar's lucky," said Loker; "fork over."

"Though the dogs might damage the gal, if they come on her unawars," said Haley.

"That ar's a consideration," said Marks. "Our dogs tore a feller half to pieces, once, down in Mobile, 'fore we could get 'em off."

"Well, ye see, for this sort that's to be sold for their looks, that ar won't answer, ye see," said Haley.

"I do see," said Marks. "Besides, if she's got took in, 'tan't no go, neither. Dogs is no 'count in these yer up states where these critters gets carried; of course, ye can't get on their track. They only does down in plantations, where when they runs, they has to do their own running, and don't get no help."…

If any of our refined and Christian readers object to the society into which this scene introduces them, let us beg them to begin and conquer their prejudices in time. The catching business, we beg to remind them, is rising to the dignity of a lawful and patriotic profession. If all the broad land between the Mississippi and the Pacific becomes one great market for bodies and souls, and human property retains the locomotive tendencies of this nineteenth century, the trader and catcher may yet be among our aristocracy.

What is the narrative point of view of this story?

A   first person (told by a character in the story)

B   third person objective (told by a narrator outside the story)

C   third person limited (told from the point of view of one character)

D   third person omniscient (revealing the thoughts of several characters)

There is no *I* in this story, and no character or characters whose minds we inhabit as the story is told. There is only an outside narrator or speaker, whose thoughts are revealed in the last paragraph. The correct answer is choice B.

How does the author develop the points of view of the three men in the tavern?

_____

_____

_____

_____

✓ Lovely fellows, aren't they, the two slave-catchers and the slave dealer who hires them? Stowe develops their characters through dialogue. Here is a sample answer:

The author shows them through their dialogue to be thoroughly offensive characters who joke about mothers loving their children as a "problem," marvel that women would care about having their children sold away from them, and consider the idea of dogs tearing into a runaway slave only as it might damage their "property."

What is the author's purpose beyond telling an entertaining story? Explain your answer giving evidence from the text.

_____

_____

_____

_____

✓ *Uncle Tom's Cabin* may not have caused the Civil War, but it did form people's opinions. Here is a sample answer:

Stowe wanted to make people feel as she did about slavery, that it was a great inhuman evil. She does this by showing the three men to be loathsome people who not only have no human feelings, but who don't understand them when they see them in others. Readers probably came to see Haley, Loker, and Marks as the "face" of slavery.

128 **UNIT 3** ▨▨▨▨▨▨▨▨▨▨▨▨▨▨▨▨▨▨▨▨▨▨▨▨▨▨▨▨▨▨▨▨▨▨▨▨
Craft and Structure

How does Stowe contrast the narrator's point of view with that of the three men?

_____

_____

_____

_____

✔ In the last paragraph, the narrator steps away from the scene to comment on it. Here, you can assume, is Stowe's voice. Here is a sample answer:

After showing you these awful creatures, Stowe comments sarcastically that if her readers are shocked and offended by them, they'd better get used to it. Catching slaves is now legal in every state, and they'll soon be seeing men like Haley, Marks, and Loker in their own communities.

How does the author's purpose and point of view influence how the three men are portrayed?

_____

_____

_____

✔ Consider for a moment that in 1850s America, these sorts of things happened all the time. Now, think of Stowe's point of view and how it is projected on the characters. Here is a sample answer:

Stowe hates slavery, and so she portrays the three men as being as nasty as possible. A Southern writer at the time might have shown Haley as an honest businessman who has been robbed, and Loker and Marks as tough detectives who are only doing their jobs.

Rethinking Uncle Tom

by T. R. Pearse

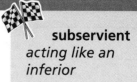

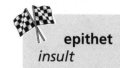

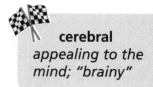

When I was growing up, during the 1970s, the worst thing you could say about an African American was to call him an Uncle Tom. The term connoted, in the words of one critic, "a subservient fool who bows down to the white man." The source of the epithet, as everyone knows, was Harriet Beecher Stowe's antislavery novel *Uncle Tom's Cabin.* The best-selling work of fiction of the 19th century, *Uncle Tom* was getting no respect in the later decades of the 20th. Black authors, from the cerebral James Baldwin to the militants of the Black Power movement, were unanimous in condemning the novel as racially obtuse, a source of condescending stereotypes that continued to damage race relations into our own day, even (I am not joking) "worse than slavery." White critics, too, were embarrassed by the novel. They called it "Sunday-school fiction"; "a blend of children's fable and propaganda"; "a singularly bad book."

I never read *Uncle Tom's Cabin* until a couple of summers ago. I was putting together a course for a community college on protest literature in American history: Tom Paine's *Common Sense,* Upton Sinclair's *The Jungle,* Rachel Carson's *The Silent Spring,* and the like. I couldn't very well teach a class like that without including the most influential piece of protest literature in our history, and so, racist though it might be, mawkish though it might be, I figured I'd better read it. Then I figured I'd better review some of the criticism, to make sure I remembered it right. Then I sat back and did some thinking.

Before I was halfway through the first chapter, I understood why few people today take *Uncle Tom's Cabin* seriously as literature. It is Sunday-school fiction, it is sentimental and melodramatic—which is only to say that it's a product of its time. If not for its historical significance, it would be as forgotten today as hundreds of other 19th-century novels, and as forgotten as most of today's best sellers will be 150 years from now. To criticize it as literature is to knock down a straw man. It's a cheap shot. It's completely irrelevant. Name one popular novel of the last 50 years that people might still be reading and discussing in 2150 as we do *Uncle Tom*.

For trashy as it is as literature, the significance of *Uncle Tom's Cabin* as a historical document cannot be dismissed, and we must confront it on its own terms. It was entirely reasonable for James Baldwin and his contemporaries to express revulsion at its stereotypes, except that in 1852 they weren't stereotypes. They were not portraits of educated black men and women of Baldwin's time or of free African Americans of Stowe's time. They were slaves, and they were survivors—and they were individuals, based on Stowe's interviews with ex-slaves, and especially on the memoirs of one Josiah Henson, her model for the character of Uncle Tom. The stereotypes—Sam the "carefree darky," Topsy the "pickaninny," Mammy the mammy, Uncle Tom the…Uncle Tom—they came later, in hundreds of adapted stage productions over which Stowe had no control. These "Tom shows" played American theaters for two generations. They cemented the stereotypes into our national consciousness. Then Hollywood took them over as stock characters in films that had no connection with the novel at all.

Thankfully, a generation has come of age that has had no exposure to the stereotypes, except perhaps in quaint old movies. Young people recognize them as demeaning and false when they see them in *Gone With the Wind*. However, when they read *Uncle Tom's Cabin*, they don't see its characters as the source of the stereotypes. They see a courageous critique of America as it was in 1852, and a book that had the power to change people's hearts and minds.

In the book, Uncle Tom is whipped on orders of the villain Simon Legree for standing up for another slave who is being abused. He is beaten to death by Legree for refusing to reveal where two runaways are hiding. Uncle Tom may have become a stereotype, but he was nobody's Uncle Tom.

> **straw man**
> *an argument or opinion set up to be easily defeated*

1 Determine the author's *main* purpose in writing this essay.

   A to answer critics of *Uncle Tom's Cabin*

   B to summarize the plot of *Uncle Tom's Cabin*

   C to persuade people to read *Uncle Tom's Cabin*

   D to explain the historical importance of *Uncle Tom's Cabin*

2   Which of these sentences *best* summarizes the author's point of view about *Uncle Tom's Cabin?*

   A   It is better than most fiction of its time.

   B   It should be read as a historical document

   C   It accurately depicts American slavery in 1852.

   D   It would be forgotten today if not for its historical importance.

3   Analyze how the author distinguishes his point of view from those of the critics quoted in the first paragraph.

   _____

   _____

   _____

   _____

   _____

4   How does the author respond to criticisms of *Uncle Tom's Cabin* as literature?

   _____

   _____

   _____

   _____

   _____

5   Examine how the language the author uses to describe *Uncle Tom's Cabin* as literature reveals his point of view.

   _____

   _____

   _____

   _____

   _____

6 What evidence does the author cite to prove that the character of Uncle Tom wasn't an "Uncle Tom"?

_____

_____

_____

_____

_____

7 How might the author have better supported his point of view about _Uncle Tom's Cabin?_

_____

_____

_____

_____

_____

8 The author believes that people today should read _Uncle Tom's Cabin_ because _____.

   A it was the best-selling work of fiction of the 19th century

   B it is the most influential piece of protest literature in our history

   C people need to decide for themselves whether or not the criticisms of the book are valid

   D young people should understand the negative stereotypes of African Americans that earlier generations were exposed to

REVIEW

Read the poem. Then answer the questions.

from Testimony

by Charles Reznikoff

Outside the night was cold, the snow was deep
on sill and sidewalk, but in our kitchen
it was bright and warm.
I smelt the damp clothes
5   as my mother lifted them from the basket,
the pungent smell of melting wax
as she rubbed it on the iron,
and the good lasting smell of meat and potatoes
in the black pot that simmered on the stove.
10 The stove was so hot it was turning red.
My mother lifted the lid of the pot
to stir the roast with a long wooden spoon:
Father would not be home for another hour.
I tugged at her skirts. Tell me a story!
15 Once upon a time (the best beginning!)
there was a rich woman, a baroness, and a poor woman, a beggar.
The poor woman came every day to beg, and every day
the rich woman gave her a loaf of bread
until the rich woman was tired of it.
20 I will put poison in the next loaf, she thought,
to be rid of her.
The beggar woman thanked the baroness for that loaf
and went to her hut,
but, as she was going through the fields,
25 she met the rich woman's son coming out of the forest.
"Hello, hello, beggar woman," said the young baron,
"I have been away for three days hunting
and am very hungry.

I know you are coming from my mother's
30 and that she has given you a loaf of bread;
let me have it—she will give you another."
"Gladly, gladly," said the beggar woman,
and, without knowing it was poisoned, gave him the loaf.
But, as he went on, he thought, I am nearly home—
35 I will wait.
You may be sure that his mother was glad to see him,
And she told the maids to bring a cup of wine
And make his supper—quickly, quickly!
"I met the beggar woman," he said,
40 "and was so hungry I asked for the loaf you gave her."
"Did you eat it, my son?" the baroness whispered.
"No, I knew you had something better for me
than this dry bread."
She threw it right into the fire,
45 And every day after that, gave the beggar woman a loaf
and never again tried to poison her.
So, my son, if you try to harm others,
you may only harm yourself.

And, mother, if you are a beggar, sooner or later,
50 there is poison in your bread.

1 Which of these *best* describes the structure of the poem?

    A   It has no line breaks between stanzas.

    B   It contains a story within another story

    C   It has repeated lines that signal the end of sections.

    D   It changes back and forth between rhymed and unrhymed verse

2 Lines 15 through 48 take the form of _____.

    A   a ballad

    B   a sonnet

    C   a folktale

    D   a limerick

3 Analyze the poem. How does the narrative point of view change?

_____

_____

_____

_____

_____

4 In lines 47–50, how does the poet contrast the points of view of the mother and child?

_____

_____

_____

_____

_____

5 Examine how the structure of the poem creates tension in lines 20–35.

_____

_____

_____

_____

_____

6 How does the poet's repetition of words and sounds change between the boy's narration and the mother's? What is the effect of this contrast on the poem?

_____

_____

_____

_____

_____

7 How does the poet's use of free verse emphasize the meaning of the poem?

_____

_____

_____

_____

_____

Read the passage. Then answer the questions.

Middle-Schoolers Make Discovery on Mars

by Ruth Stock

Students in a seventh-grade science class discovered a cave on Mars in 2010 without leaving their classroom in Cottonwood, California. The 16 students in Mr. Dennis Mitchell's science class at Evergreen Middle School found the cave by spotting a hole in the roof, like a skylight, in a photo taken by a NASA spacecraft orbiting Mars.

The students were participating in a research project called the Mars Student Imaging Program (MSIP), run by the Mars Space Flight Facility at Arizona State University. The program allows students from fifth grade through second-year college to propose questions for scientific study of the red planet. The students can commission photographs from the facility to aid them in answering their questions. The photos are taken by a camera

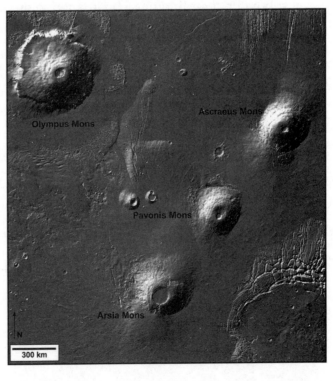

on board the *Mars Odyssey,* a spacecraft that orbits Mars every two hours. Student teams network with the facility's scientists from their classrooms by videoconferencing or the Internet, giving them the chance to get advice from experts, but they have to do the research themselves. For some projects, students get to spend three days at the facility in Arizona working with the professional staff. For all MSIP projects, the students are the first to see the images of Mars that they have commissioned.

The Evergreen seventh graders had designed a project to find lava tubes, which occur in conjunction with volcanoes on both Earth and Mars. Lava flows from erupting volcanoes carve out underground channels in rock. When the eruption is over, the channels remain as tunnels covered by a solid ceiling of cooling rock. The question the students wanted to investigate was whether these tubes most often occur near the summit of a volcano, on its slopes, or on the plains around it. They commissioned a main photo and a backup of a Martian volcano called Pavonis Mons, focusing on an area that not previously been photographed up close. Both pictures showed lava tubes. But the backup photo also showed a small, round black spot: a hole leading into a cave.

The Evergreen students shared their discovery with Glen Cushing, a scientist with the U.S. Geological Survey, who in 2007 discovered seven similar features associated with caves on different parts of Mars. His hypothesis is that they are places where part of the roof of a lava tube collapsed. Cushing assured the students that their cave had previously been unknown to science and was only the second discovered near Pavonis Mons. He estimated the cave to be at least 380 feet deep and about 620 by 520 feet wide.

Scientists don't know what type of minerals might be found in these caves, but they may soon have some ideas. The Evergreen students have submitted their finding to be imaged in greater detail by another NASA camera orbiting Mars.

"The Mars Student Imaging Program is certainly one of the greatest educational programs ever developed," teacher Dennis Mitchell commented. "It gives the students a good understanding of the way research is conducted and how that research can be important for the scientific community. This has been a wonderful experience."

8 Which of these *best* describes the author's purpose in writing this article?

A to explain a problem and an attempt to solve it

B to describe how students made a discovery on Mars

C to explain the procedure the students used to discover the cave

D to persuade students and teachers to apply for the MSIP program

9 Which of these *best* describes the structure the author used to organize her information?

    A causes and effects

    B order of importance

    C questions and answers

    D comparison and contrast

10 How does paragraph 2 help you to better understand the ideas in the article?

_____

_____

_____

_____

_____

11 What is the question the author is seeking to answer with the information in paragraph 3? What is an important point about science that she makes in this paragraph?

_____

_____

_____

_____

_____

12 How does the way the students' teacher comments about the program compare and contrast with the point of view expressed by the author? Explain how and why.

_____

_____

_____

_____

_____

13 Paragraph 4 *mainly* contributes to the ideas in the article by _____.

    A giving facts and figures about the cave

    B providing additional data about caves on Mars

    C relating the students' finding to previous research

    D explaining what a professional scientist thought about the discovery

14 Explain how the author's use of the word *research* affects the tone of the article.

_____

_____

_____

_____

_____

UNIT 3 ▨▨▨▨▨▨▨▨▨▨▨▨▨▨▨▨▨▨▨▨▨▨▨▨▨▨▨▨▨▨
Craft and Structure

Integration of Knowledge and Ideas

Reading and understanding can involve piecing together information from several sources, fiction as well as nonfiction. Sometimes these sources may be visual rather than verbal. Reading several texts on the same topic can give you a deeper perspective than a single text. It can also give you insights about the accuracy of the information you're reading, as you weigh evidence presented in one text against the points made in another, and as you consider which details in a fictional account of an event are true and which the creation of the author. Visual aids, too, such as photographs, maps, graphs, and diagrams, can enhance your understanding of what you're reading. In literary texts, noting similarities among topics and themes and the different ways authors approach them can add to your enjoyment and understanding of what you read.

This unit is about how you absorb information and piece together ideas from several sources to come up with new insights and ideas.

● **In Lesson 11,** you'll learn how visual elements can add meaning and depth to texts about history and science and can help you find answers to questions and solutions to problems related to the topic.

● **Lesson 12** is about reasons and evidence in informational text. You'll learn how to distinguish among facts, opinions, and reasoned judgment and how to evaluate which specific points the author is making are based on reasons and evidence.

● **Lesson 13** is about comparing and contrasting different texts on similar themes and topics. You'll learn how authors of historical fiction can deal with themes of history with more freedom and imagination than fact-based authors, and how a secondary source on a topic can make use of one or more primary sources in ways that can give you better insight and understanding than a single text.

Visual Literacy

RI.7.7, RH.7.7, RST.7.7

Vocabulary

besieged
endemic
eradication
infrastructure
refracted
shenanigans

Images and sound can often give you insights about what you're reading that words alone cannot. Seeing a play performed on a stage or hearing a poem read aloud is a different experience than reading it silently. An illustration can let you picture characters and settings more vividly. The effect can be even greater in a filmed version of a story, where lighting and camera angles can help determine the way you feel about a character or setting. Visual material such as illustrations, photographs, maps, diagrams, charts, and graphs give information on a nonfiction topic or idea in ways that enhance your understanding of the text. It's the same with your ears as with your eyes. Hearing a recording of Martin Luther King's "I Have a Dream" speech is a more powerful experience that reading it in a book.

Guided Practice

Read the passage. Then answer the questions.

A Photographic Eye

by Edward Seaton

Have you ever noticed how many human inventions mimic functions of the human body? Some can even be considered extensions of it. When computers were new, people often called them "electronic brains." Indeed, the circuitry of a computer, its input and processing functions and its memory, parallel the way our brain and central nervous system work. Likewise, a lever confers mechanical advantage like our bones and muscles do, and some machine parts operate on the same principles as our knees, shoulders, and other joints.

The human eye is so like a camera in its structure and function that it is logical to compare and contrast them. Both have two essential parts: a **lens system** and an **imaging sensor.** In the eye, the imaging sensor is the **retina.** In a modern digital camera, it's a light-sensitive system of electronics on a silicon chip, called a charge-coupled device, or **CCD.** In a traditional camera, the imaging sensor is a strip of film or a plate coated with chemicals. Between the lens and the sensor is a substance that allows light to pass through without interference. In a camera the substance is air; in the eye it's a transparent liquid.

Does your family have an old, broken camera? If you can get permission, carefully disassemble it with a group so that you can see all the parts. Can you figure out what made it stop working?

In both an eye and a camera, the job of the lens is to focus light on the imaging sensor. Light reflected off what you see (or what the camera is pointed at) is refracted through the lens so that the image appears on the sensor. If the lens system is in focus, every point of what you see (or what the camera "sees") will have a corresponding point on the imaging sensor. If it's not in focus, a point of light will project as a circular area—the image will be blurry. On a camera, you can correct the focus by moving the lens toward or away from the imaging sensor. A "point-and-shoot" camera does this automatically, and so do your eyes. The lens in each eye is actually a pair of convex lenses, one behind the other, with transparent liquid between them. It's the inner lens that automatically adjusts, controlled by muscles in the eye. When these muscles contract, the lens flattens, bringing the image into focus on the retina.

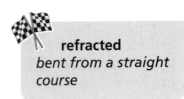

refracted
bent from a straight course

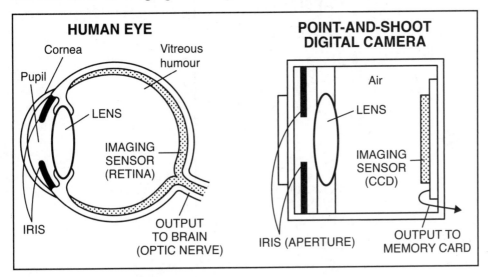

Human Eye and Camera   **Diagram 1**

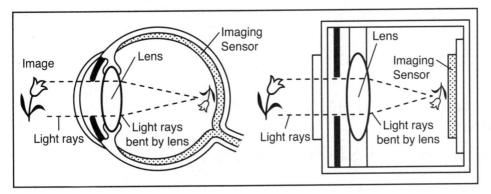

Refraction   **Diagram 2**

Both the eye and the camera have an **iris** that controls how much light goes through the lens. In your eyes, the iris is made up of muscle tissue that expands and contracts, changing the size of the pupil, or light opening. In a camera the iris is mechanical, but it does exactly the same job.

When light is projected onto the imaging sensor, whether it's a retina, a CCD, or a strip of film, it needs to be processed into a form that you can perceive. Your eyes do this by passing the image along fibers that lead to the optic nerve and then to the brain. In a digital camera, the CCD translates the image into a pattern of voltage levels that correspond to the amount of light that has fallen on each tiny picture element. This pattern is stored on a memory card, where the camera or a computer can retrieve it and convert it back into a visual image.

Mechanical or electronic systems can be made more precise than nature. In some people, the lens is too close to the retina, so that the image focuses behind the eye. In others the lens and retina are too far apart, so that the image focuses in front of the eye. You can't make your eyeball longer or shorter, but you can improve the focus by adding artificial lenses. You may be wearing a pair right now.

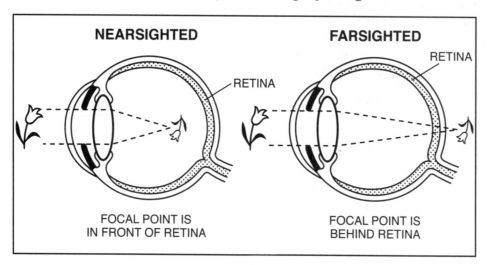

Nearsightedness and Farsightedness   **Diagram 3**

Which sentence in the article is *best* illustrated by the first pair of diagrams on page 143?

A In both an eye and a camera, the job of the lens is to focus light on the imaging sensor.

B Both the eye and the camera have an iris that controls how much light goes through the lens.

C Between the lens and the sensor is a substance that allows light to pass through without interference.

D The human eye is so like a camera in its structure and function that it is logical to compare and contrast them.

The first pair of diagrams illustrates the main idea of the article: the similarities and differences in structure and function between the human eye and the camera. Comparing and contrasting them is what the article mainly does. Everything else is a supporting idea, like answer choices A, B and C. The correct answer is choice D.

UNIT 4 ▓▓▓
Integration of Knowledge and Ideas

The first pair of diagrams helps you see that in the eye, the iris is located _____.

A   behind the lens

B   in front of the lens

C   behind the imaging sensor

D   in front of the imaging sensor

The article tells you that the job of the iris is to control the amount of light that gets through the lens. It makes sense that it could be any place but behind the imaging sensor. However, in the human eye it happens to be directly in front of the lens. (Is it the same or different with the camera?) Choice B is the correct answer.

What part of the eye corresponds to the air that fills the camera?

_____

_____

The article explains that the substance between the lens and the imaging sensor must be transparent so that light can pass through without interference. The article calls the substance in the eye "a transparent liquid," but the diagram shows you its scientific name. Here is a sample answer:

The part of the eye that corresponds to the air that fills the camera is the vitreous humor.

What does the second pair of diagrams on page 143 illustrate? How does it help you understand the meaning of *refracted?*

_____

_____

_____

_____

 The second pair of diagrams also compares and contrasts a function of the eye and the camera: how the lens focuses an image on the imaging sensor. Here is a sample answer:

> These diagrams show how what you see and what a camera sees is focused by the lens system. It shows you that light from the images is bent through the lens so that the image appears in reverse on the imaging sensor, and "bent" is what refracted means.

When a person needs glasses or contact lenses for nearsightedness, it's because _____.

    A   the retina is not directly behind the lens

    B   the iris does not open and close properly

    C   the lens focuses an image behind the retina

    D   the lens focuses an image in front of the retina

 The third pair of diagrams shows what causes nearsightedness and farsightedness. Choice C defines farsightedness, while choices A and B are more serious vision problems that glasses or contacts wouldn't correct. Choice D is the correct answer.

How do the visual materials in this article help you understand the way the eye and the camera work?

_____

_____

_____

_____

 Read the passage again, this time covering up the diagrams with your hand or a sheet of paper. It's harder to understand, isn't it, even though you're reading it for the second time? Answers to this question may vary widely. Here is a sample answer:

The diagrams help explain what the different parts are and the relationships between them. They show you what's similar and what's different between the eye and a camera, and what the lens focusing an image on the imaging sensor actually means.

Read the passage. Then answer the questions.

Marching Through Georgia

by Paul B. Williams

infrastructure
physical and organizational structures and services, such as roads and water supply

Modern warfare, some historians have said, began on November 15, 1864. That was when Union General William T. Sherman, whose army had occupied the Southern city of Atlanta, Georgia, in September, ordered the city burned and began his march to Savannah and the sea.

The American Civil War by then had been raging for nearly four years and claimed hundreds of thousands of lives, North and South. Union armies had pushed deep into the Confederate states, and there was no longer any doubt that the North would win. Still, the South would not give in, and as long as they were willing to fight, the dying would continue. Sherman and his commander, Ulysses S. Grant, decided that the South would quit only when its ability to make war was destroyed. That meant a strategy of "total war"—destroying the South's economy, its infrastructure, and the will of its people. Sherman was willing to apply that strategy to Georgia.

"We cannot change the hearts of these people of the South," he said, "but we can make war so terrible…and make them so sick of war that generations will pass away before they again appeal to it."

He began by ordering all civilians out of Atlanta. He meant to burn the city so that the Southern army and people would not have its resources to fall back on. When the mayor and city council protested, Sherman sent a famous reply:

Gentlemen: You cannot qualify war in harsher terms than I will. War is cruelty and you cannot refine it…. You cannot have peace and a division of our country. You may as well appeal against the thunderstorm as against these terrible hardships of war.

The people of Georgia were soon to taste those hardships.

Sherman divided his army into two great columns, 62,000 men in all. Against them the South could only spare 13,000 troops, since most of its army, under General Robert E. Lee, was besieged by Grant in Petersburg, Virginia. With no way to supply his armies on the march, Sherman's orders were to "live off the land": to take what they needed from farms. Anywhere they met with opposition or obstruction, they were given license to seize livestock as they needed it and otherwise to destroy utterly any houses, factories, roads, bridges, railroads, and other property in their path.

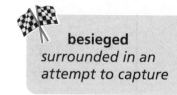

besieged
surrounded in an attempt to capture

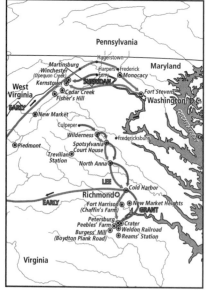

Lee and Grant

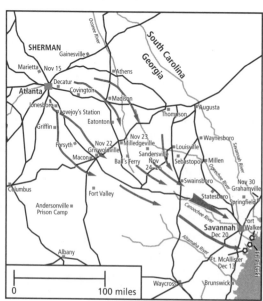

Sherman's march to the sea

UNIT 4 ▚▚▚▚▚▚▚▚▚▚▚▚▚▚▚▚▚▚▚▚▚▚▚▚▚▚▚
Integration of Knowledge and Ideas

They met with little opposition. "This is probably the greatest pleasure excursion ever planned," wrote one of Sherman's soldiers. Another boasted of how they "Destroyed all we could not eat, stole their [slaves], burned their cotton...burned and twisted their railroads..." A woman whose farm was in their path remembered how they had rushed in "Like demons...! To my smokehouse, my dairy, pantry, kitchen and cellar, like famished wolves they come, breaking locks and whatever is in their way." Along the line of march, few buildings were left standing. Whatever animals Sherman's army could not eat or use to pull their wagons, they shot.

"The cruelties practiced on this campaign toward the citizens," wrote a Union soldier, "have been enough to blast a more sacred cause than ours. We hardly deserve success."

Privately, Sherman agreed. However, on December 22, he sent Abraham Lincoln a telegram: "I beg to present you, as a Christmas gift, the city of Savannah...."

A few weeks later, Sherman's army turned north along the coast, devastating the Carolinas as they had Georgia. By April, the war was over. Its scars remain to this day in Georgia, where the name of Sherman is still a curse.

Based on information in the article, what does the photograph on page 148 show? What question does it raise in your mind?

_____

_____

_____

 The Civil War was the first war in history to be well documented by photographs. Here is a sample answer:

The photograph shows the devastation and destruction of the war. It shows railroads being torn up. The photograph makes you wonder what happened to the people and how they survived.

The photograph *best* illustrates which of these sentences from the article?

A War is cruelty and you cannot refine it.

B Modern warfare, historians have said, began on November 15, 1864.

C Sherman divided his army into two great columns, 62,000 men in all.

D The American Civil War by then had been raging for nearly four years and claimed hundreds of thousands of lives, North and South.

The photo does illustrate "modern warfare," the destruction wrought by the Civil War, and what can happen when an army passes through with orders to seize and destroy. However, it best illustrates Sherman's reply to the mayor of Atlanta. The correct answer is choice A.

On the map on page 148 of Sherman's March, what do the names like "Ball's Ferry" and "Grahamville" with accompanying dates represent?

They could be the names of towns, but what about the place names that don't have dates below them? Here is a sample answer:

They are places and dates where battles were fought.

Determine how the map supports the information about the destruction that took place along the march.

Here is a sample answer:

The map shows that the march was about 300 miles long from Atlanta to the sea, and that the army was divided into groups that spread over an area about 60 miles wide. That's about 18,000 square miles that looked something like the scene in the photograph.

UNIT 4 ▨▨▨▨▨▨▨▨▨▨▨▨▨▨▨▨▨▨▨▨▨▨▨▨▨▨▨▨▨▨▨▨▨▨▨
Integration of Knowledge and Ideas

The Canal and the Mosquito

by Frank Maltesi

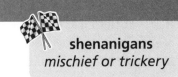

shenanigans
mischief or trickery

It was the most ambitious engineering project ever conceived, and it was almost done in before it was properly started. A canal across the Isthmus of Panama had been in the mind of U.S. President Theodore Roosevelt since the Spanish-American War, when the battleship *Oregon* had had to make a 71-day journey around the tip of South America before going into action. It had cost a great deal of money and considerable political shenanigans to obtain the rights to dig the Panama Canal through 50 miles of jungle, swamp, and mountains. The first steam-shovelful of earth was excavated in 1904. By 1905, the engineers were almost ready to abandon the project.

The reason was yellow fever. It was a disease that killed in vile, horrible ways. It had been endemic in Panama for 250 years, and had plagued the United States for almost as long. An epidemic in 1793 had killed ten percent of the population of Philadelphia and caused President George Washington and his cabinet to flee the city. An epidemic in 1878 had spread through the Mississippi Valley from New Orleans to Memphis, killing 20,000 Americans. It was in the tropical lands of Africa and Latin America that this terrifying disease did its worst work. A French company had tried to dig a canal through Panama in the 1880s. After ten years and the deaths of 22,000 workers from yellow fever, the project had been abandoned.

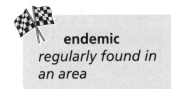

endemic
regularly found in an area

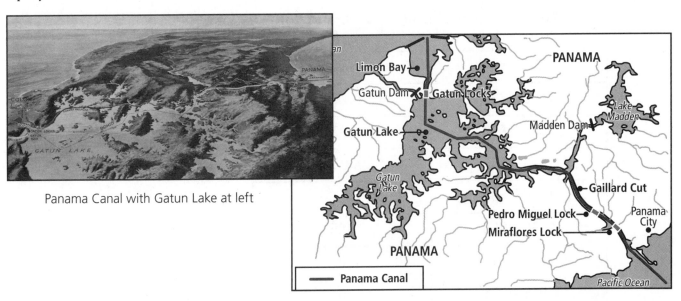

Panama Canal with Gatun Lake at left

Panama Canal with locks that control water levels

Now, only a few months into the American canal project, 47 workers had succumbed to the "black vomit." One of the horrors of the disease was that no one seemed to know what caused it. Was it contagious? Did it arise out of the foul air of tropical swamps? The bacterial origins of some diseases had been well known for a generation, but microscopic study of the bodily fluids of yellow-fever victims did not reveal a cause.

In fact, it was not quite true that no one knew the cause of the disease. In Cuba, where yellow fever was even a greater scourge than in Panama, a doctor named Carlos Finlay in 1881 had proposed the theory that the disease was spread by a certain type of mosquito. Few people had paid attention. Then during the Spanish-American war, with yellow fever killing far more American soldiers and sailors in Cuba than combat, Dr. Walter Reed conducted experiments that proved Finlay was right. Another doctor, William Gorgas, led a mosquito-eradication project in Cuba's capital city of Havana. The results were dramatic. In 1900, 1,400 people in Havana had died of yellow fever. The mosquito-eradication project began in February 1901. That year, 37 people died of the disease. The following year, there were none.

eradication
wiping out

In 1905, Reed and Gorgas applied Dr. Finlay's methods to Panama. Within a year, yellow fever had been eradicated from the Canal Zone, and from Panama. The abatement program also cut in half the cases of another mosquito-borne disease, malaria. The Panama Canal project still faced obstacles, but now they were mostly geographical.

As for yellow fever, 1905 saw the end of history's last U.S. epidemic, in New Orleans. Since then, only one person has died from a case of the disease caught in the United States, in 1924. In 1927, it was discovered that the disease is actually caused by a virus carried by the mosquito. A vaccine was soon developed. Yellow fever is still a problem in some countries, particularly in Africa. However, wherever mosquito eradication and widespread vaccination has been in effect, the disease has disappeared.

Yellow Fever—Before and After Mosquito Control
Data from the city of New Orleans, 1856–1925

Years	Yellow Fever Deaths
1856–1865	5,236
1866–1875	4,224
1876–1885	4,068
1886–1895	1
1896–1905	885
1906–1915	0
1916–1925	0

Integration of Knowledge and Ideas

1 Determine which fact in the article is emphasized by the map of North and South America on page 151.

_____

_____

_____

_____

_____

2 Compare the photograph and map of the Panama Canal Zone. How do they show how difficult building the canal was? How do they show how engineers solved the problem of building a canal through mountains?

_____

_____

_____

_____

_____

3 How do the maps show you why Theodore Roosevelt and others wanted to build the canal?

_____

_____

_____

_____

_____

4 Explain how the table on page 152 proves Dr. Finlay's theory about the cause of yellow fever.

_____

_____

_____

_____

_____

5 The table on page 152 shows 4,068 deaths from yellow fever in New Orleans between the years 1876–1885. In what year would most of those deaths have taken place? Explain why, using information from the article.

_____

_____

_____

_____

_____

6 How would you explain the number on the table from 1886–1895?

_____

_____

_____

_____

_____

Identifying Connections

RI.7.8, RH.7.8, RST.7.8

Vocabulary
docile
exponentially
purported

When you read nonfiction, you assume that you are reading facts. The only exception is when the author plainly is trying to persuade you to buy or believe something. You expect an editorial or critical review to contain the author's opinions, and you know that you should use your reasoned judgment when reading an advertisement. Sometimes, however, what you think is fact may actually be someone else's judgment, or even an opinion dressed up as fact.

What's the difference? A **fact** is a statement that is supported by evidence. If the author doesn't cite her sources, there are places where you can check for yourself. For example, if a news article states that your city's oldest movie theater has just closed down, there are likely to be old documents in the city library that confirm that the theater was indeed built in 1907.

Reasoned judgment or **speculation** may be a conclusion based on evidence, but it is not solidly supported by evidence. Suppose a science article about some recently discovered fossil bones states that "Dr. Joan Pell of the County Museum of Science affirms that the bones are probably those of an ice-age mammoth that lived about 15,500 years ago." You can assume that Dr. Pell is reasoning based on comparison of the bones with other mammoth remains, and you know that there are reliable dating methods that scientists use to determine the age of fossils. A statement can be assumed to be true if there is a well-established method for determining its accuracy. If other scientists' reasoned judgment tells them that Dr. Pell made a mistake in her methods, you can be sure that they'll challenge her conclusions.

An **opinion** is not supported by evidence at all. It tells you how the author, or someone else, thinks and feels about a subject. Judgmental words like *best* or *worst* can show that someone is expressing an opinion. So can generalizations that use words like *everyone, nobody, always,* or *never*. Or, it could be that an author is simply making a statement that he would like to be true and is presenting it as if it were true. If someone says, "Those bones are fakes" because he just doesn't care to believe that mammoths were walking around 15,500 years ago, he's just stating an opinion. A judgment based on what someone would like to believe is not a reasoned judgment at all.

As you read, ask yourself "What is the evidence?" Your own reasoned judgment can serve as a "baloney detector." Pay attention to the points the author makes. Is information presented as fact backed up with evidence? How convincing is the evidence? Is it from a primary source, such as an on-the-spot account of a historic event or a scientist's data? Or, is it from a secondary source, like a historian's interpretation of the event or a summary of the experiment by a nonscientist? Does the source know what she's talking about, or is he just exercising his right of free speech? Are you reading complete information, or is the author leaving out facts that don't support her opinions? Is the information up to date, or are you reading old "facts" that time has turned into fiction? Does the author clearly favor one side of an argument even though he pretends to be fair and balanced in his opinions? Asking yourself questions like these when you read for information will help you distinguish among fact, opinion, and reasoned judgment.

Guided Practice

Read the passage. Then answer the questions.

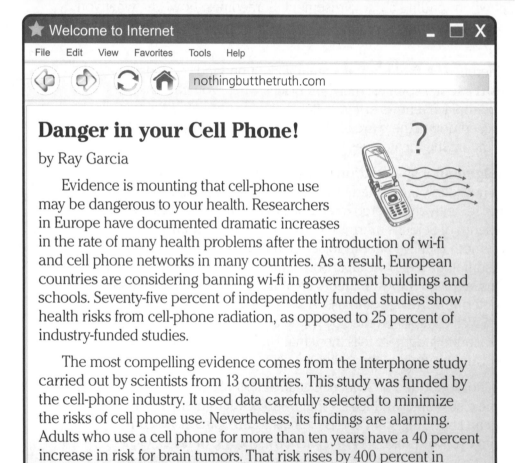

Danger in your Cell Phone!

by Ray Garcia

Evidence is mounting that cell-phone use may be dangerous to your health. Researchers in Europe have documented dramatic increases in the rate of many health problems after the introduction of wi-fi and cell phone networks in many countries. As a result, European countries are considering banning wi-fi in government buildings and schools. Seventy-five percent of independently funded studies show health risks from cell-phone radiation, as opposed to 25 percent of industry-funded studies.

The most compelling evidence comes from the Interphone study carried out by scientists from 13 countries. This study was funded by the cell-phone industry. It used data carefully selected to minimize the risks of cell phone use. Nevertheless, its findings are alarming. Adults who use a cell phone for more than ten years have a 40 percent increase in risk for brain tumors. That risk rises by 400 percent in people who start using a cell phone before the age of 20.

The United States did not participate in the Interphone study. The U.S. government has for 50 years actively suppressed data on the risks of microwave radiation, such as is emitted by cell phones. An industry group, the Institute of Electrical and Electronics Engineers (IEEE), determines what standards of radiation exposure are considered safe. Microwave radiation, as everyone knows, can cook food. Yet, we routinely hold sources of that radiation up against our ears!

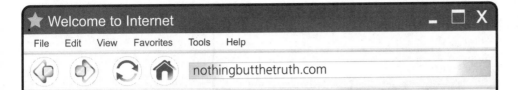

Despite the enforced silence, people are becoming aware of the dangers of cell-phone use. An anonymous banker, speaking to a reporter from *GQ* magazine, reported that the rates of brain-tumor use are "shockingly high," and that more and more people are blaming constant cell-phone use. "I know four or five people just at my firm who got tumors," according to the banker. "Each time, people ask the question. I hear it in the hallways."

It took more than 30 years for the public to get angry enough about the connection between smoking and lung cancer to demand action on the issue. How long will it be before we awaken to the danger of cell phones?

All comments posted on this site is commentary or opinion and protected as free speech. Nothingbutthetruth.com takes sole responsibility for all content.

I am a physics teacher, not connected with the government or the cell-phone industry. Yes, cell phones emit microwaves. They produce heat. You hold it close to your brain. The fact is they use a very, very low level of radio frequency energy—too low to cause damage. The energy they emit is nonionizing—meaning it cannot damage chemical bonds or DNA.
Posted 10/12/10 12:47 pm by GeorgeB

Are we surprised? Government and industry have been working together to poison us for 60 years. Sure, they've suppressed the data. They want us docile and weak, the more easily to gouge us of our money and our freedom. Wake up, America.
Posted 10/13/10 1:59 am by TruePatriot

docile
tame; gentle

Read the Interphone study a little more critically, Ray. The margin of error for their data on cell phones and brain tumors is so large as to make their findings inconclusive. It also states that brain-cancer rates and deaths have actually *declined* in the last ten years, a time during which cell phone use has increased exponentially.
Posted 10/14/10 8:45 am by Marisa

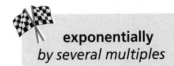

exponentially
by several multiples

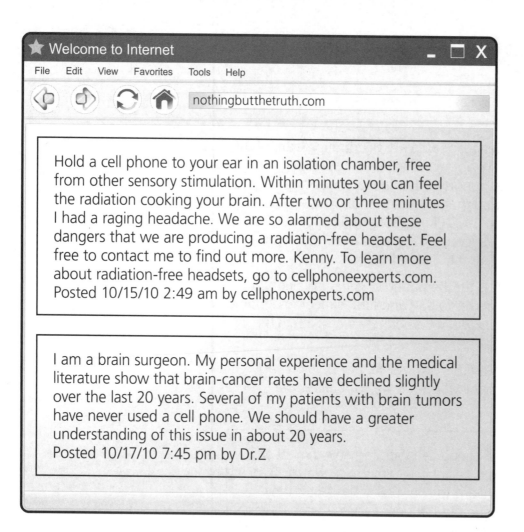

Hold a cell phone to your ear in an isolation chamber, free from other sensory stimulation. Within minutes you can feel the radiation cooking your brain. After two or three minutes I had a raging headache. We are so alarmed about these dangers that we are producing a radiation-free headset. Feel free to contact me to find out more. Kenny. To learn more about radiation-free headsets, go to cellphoneexperts.com.
Posted 10/15/10 2:49 am by cellphonexperts.com

I am a brain surgeon. My personal experience and the medical literature show that brain-cancer rates have declined slightly over the last 20 years. Several of my patients with brain tumors have never used a cell phone. We should have a greater understanding of this issue in about 20 years.
Posted 10/17/10 7:45 pm by Dr.Z

Determine which of these statements about the Interphone study is an opinion.

A The results of the Interphone study are alarming.

B The Interphone study was funded by the cell-phone industry.

C The United States did not participate in the Interphone study.

D The Interphone study was carried out by scientists from 13 countries.

Which of these statements is not supported by evidence or by reasoning from fact? You could find out which countries' scientists were involved in the Interphone study (it has been published on the Internet with many graphs, tables of data, and commentary), and a little digging could tell you whether money for the study came from the electronics industry. However, it's only Garcia's opinion that the results are "alarming." The physicist and brain surgeon who commented on his blog post don't seem to be alarmed. Choice A is the correct answer.

Ray Garcia begins his blog post with the statement, "Evidence is mounting that cell-phone use may be dangerous to your health." Does his reasoning and the evidence he presents support this claim? Explain why, or why not.

_____

_____

_____

_____

_____

_____

Ray Garcia claims to offer evidence that cell-phone use can cause brain tumors. However, at second glance, it's not convincing. He doesn't tell you where his data comes from except for mentioning one study, which one of his readers says he hasn't interpreted correctly. What "health problems" and "health risks" is he specifically talking about in his first paragraph? Does any evidence link them with cell-phone use, or did they just happen at about the same time? What countries are "considering" banning cell phones in government buildings and schools? Here is a sample answer:

Garcia's post does not support his claim. He doesn't present any evidence, just vague statements that give no specific details. He gives details on one study, but he doesn't show the data, and he doesn't offer any expert opinion that the study means what he says it does. At the end of his post is a statement that everything he says on his post is "comment or opinion protected as free speech"—not fact or even reasoned judgment.

Read this statement from the passage.

An industry group, the Institute of Electrical and Electronics Engineers (IEEE), determines what standards of radiation exposure are considered safe.

Is this statement fact, opinion, or reasoned judgment? Explain why.

_____

_____

_____

 The question is not "Is cell-phone radiation dangerous?" but "Who decides what levels of cell-phone radiation are safe?" Here is a sample answer:

> This statement is a fact. It's something you could look up with the help of a reference librarian. It's either true or it isn't, so it's not a matter of judgment from reasoning or of what Mr. Garcia believes.

Is the statement by the banker quoted in paragraph 4 to be taken as evidence in support of Garcia's point? Explain why, or why not.

_____

_____

_____

_____

 How does the banker know that brain-tumor rates are high? How high is "shockingly"? Do "four or five people" in one office show that brain-tumor rates are high? Does the banker show that they were caused by cell-phone use? Do "more and more people" represent evidence? Here is a sample answer:

> Nothing in the banker's statement represents relevant evidence or reasoned judgment. Neither he nor the "more and more people" who talk about it "in the hallways" are reasoning from evidence. They may reasonably be scared that something in their office environment is causing brain tumors, but it's only people's opinions that it has anything to do with cell phones.

UNIT 4 ❊❊
Integration of Knowledge and Ideas

Which of the comments following Garcia's post is *best* supported by evidence? Which is the *least* supported? Explain why.

_____

_____

_____

_____

_____

_____

_____

✓ You do read some interesting comments on the Internet! It's up to you to use your reasoned judgment to decide whose statements are supported by relevant evidence and whose are not. "GeorgeB" and "Dr.Z" may or may not be who they say they are, but consider what they say in support of their statements. Here is a sample answer:

Marisa's post is best supported by evidence. She cites the same study that Garcia does, but she says that the data are inconclusive and that Garcia is interpreting them incorrectly. One of her points, that brain tumors have declined as cell phone use has increased, is also supported by Dr. Z's statement. The least reliable is cellphoneexperts.com. He's trying to sell you one of his magic headsets, and I don't know anyone who feels like his brain is cooking when he uses a cell phone.

Based on Garcia's post and the comments that follow, what conclusions can you draw about the dangers of brain tumors from cell-phone use? Explain why.

_____

_____

_____

_____

_____

_____

_____

_____

✓ To answer this question, you need to weigh all the facts, opinions, and reasoned judgments reported by the author and the other posters, consider facts that he doesn't include, and apply your own reasoned judgment. There are many reasonable answers. Here is a sample answer:

Everyone agrees that cell phones emit microwaves. The question is whether they are dangerous. Some studies seem to indicate that they are, especially those that are independently funded and not supported by the electronics industry, but Garcia doesn't present evidence from any of them. The one study he does cite is interpreted differently by Marisa. Even so, it makes you think about how much you should use a cell phone. It may be, as "Dr.Z" writes, that we'll know better in 20 years, but I use a cell phone now. I'd like to see someone explain the results of more of the studies, and explain them better than Garcia did.

Test Yourself

The Beale Treasure

by Frank Maltesi

In the Appalachian foothills of southern Virginia lies buried treasure worth two million dollars. At least that's what a lot of people believe. Dozens of treasure seekers have dug up the woods of Bedford County looking for iron pots containing gold, silver, and jewels. Hundreds more have pored over the pages of coded numbers said to hold the secret of the treasure.

The treasure hunt began in 1885, when a Virginia man named James B. Ward began selling copies of a pamphlet, "The Beale Papers." It purported to tell the story of one Thomas Jefferson Beale. According to the pamphlet, in 1817 Beale had led a hunting party of 30 men to what is now New Mexico. While tracking buffalo, they discovered a rich vein of gold and silver. In 1819 and again in 1821, Beale brought some of the riches back by wagon. On both trips, Beale stayed at an inn in what today is the town of Montvale, Virginia. The inn was owned by a man named Robert Morriss.

purported
claimed

In the spring of 1822, according to Ward's pamphlet, Beale left for the west again. He left a locked iron box with Morriss for safekeeping. Beale told Morriss that if he could not return for the box, he would send him a letter instructing him what to do with it. Neither Beale nor any of his hunting partners were ever seen again. Morriss never received Beale's promised letter.

It was 23 years before Morriss forced open the box. There he found three sheets of paper filled with numbers, along with a message addressed to him from Beale. The message described how the treasure was found. It explained that the pages of numbers were codes. One revealed the location of the treasure. The second described the treasure in detail. The third was a list of names and addresses of the men on the hunting trip who were to share in the treasure. The codes were simple ciphers in which each number stood for a letter. They had been constructed using a "book key." That is, the numbers referred to the sequence of letters in a certain book. But what book? Morriss supposed that the letter Beale had promised to send him would have contained that information.

Morriss tried for the rest of his life to break the code. Just before his death in 1862, he passed the code on to a friend. We do not know the name of this friend. Supposedly, he spent the rest of *his* life trying to find the treasure, too, going broke and driving away his family in the process.

However, before he died, this man broke the code of the second page. The "book key" was the Declaration of Independence. Each number in the code corresponded to the first letter of a word in the Declaration. The number 6, for example, meant *h*, the first letter of the document's sixth word, "human." The message detailed the treasure and how it was buried. There were more than 2,000 pounds of gold and 5,000 of silver. There were jewels that Beale had obtained in trade in St. Louis to save transportation. They were buried in two separate places, packed in iron pots in holes lined with stone.

All of this information first came to light in Ward's pamphlet. Ward said he had obtained it from Morriss' friend, whose name he never revealed.

The Beale Cipher

Here is the beginning of the page of code that was deciphered using the Declaration of Independence:

115 73 24 807 37 52 49 17 31 62 647 22 7 15 140 47 29
107 79 84 56 239 10 26 811 5 196 308 85 52 160 136 59
211 36 9 46 316 554 122 106 95 53 58 2 42 7 35 122 53
31 82 77 250 196 56 96 118 71 140 287 28 353 37 1005
65 147 807 24 3 8 12 47 43 59 807 45 316 101 41 78 154
1005 122 138 191 16 77 49 102 57 72 34 73 85 35 371
59 196 81 92 191 106 273 60 394 620 270 220 106 388
287 63 3 6 191 122 43 234 400 106…

Ever since, people have sought to discover what "books" hold the key to the other pages. They have scrutinized the U.S. Constitution and the speeches of Thomas Jefferson. They have studied the books of the Bible and the plays of William Shakespeare. One seeker obtained copies of an 1821 newspaper that Beale might have seen in Morriss' inn. The codes have never been broken.

From the beginning, there were those who declared that the Beale code was a fake. Code experts were suspicious of the ways the ciphers were constructed. Some parts were apparently coded with great care, others carelessly. The page that's supposed to contain 30 names and addresses appears far too short. The Beale letters, supposedly written in the 1820s, included several words such as stampede and improvise that were not in use before the 1840s.

A writer named Peter Viemeister did some detective work on the story. He found that there were two Thomas Jefferson Beales, father and son, living in that part of Virginia in the early 1800s. The father had wounded a man in a duel in 1806 and left quickly for New Orleans. The son apparently followed him there in 1818 and died in New Orleans in 1823. The man wounded in the duel was named James Risque. He turns out to have been the grandfather of—James B. Ward. Ward himself seems to have left no record of his existence in Virginia, with one exception. He is listed as the owner of a house in which a 77-year-old woman died in 1865. Her name was given as Sarah Morriss—once the wife of Robert Morriss.

However, $20 million in treasure has an appeal that has lasted through the years. In 2001, a man claimed on the Internet to have decoded one of the two remaining cipher texts and found one of Beale's hiding places. Alas, the treasure was not there, and neither was any explanation of the cipher. Among those who have taken the treasure seriously was William Friedman. He was the director of the government's enemy code-breaking operation during World War II and perhaps the greatest code expert in American history.

1 Determine which of these statements is an opinion.

  A Thomas Jefferson Beale was a real person.

  B James Ward owned the house where Robert Morriss's wife died.

  C Ward began the treasure hunt with a pamphlet he published in 1885.

  D James Ward obtained the information in his pamphlet from Robert Morriss's friend.

2 Which of these *best* summarizes the author's thoughts about the Beale treasure?

  A It is his reasoned judgment that the Beale pamphlet was a fake.

  B It is his opinion that anyone who goes hunting for hidden treasure is pursuing a foolish dream.

  C The fact that serious code experts consider the Beale treasure to be real is evidence of its existence.

  D The fact that no one has broken the two ciphers or found the treasure is evidence that it does not exist.

3 Explain your answer to question 2.

_____

_____

_____

_____

4 Read this statement from the passage.

Some parts of the cipher were coded with great care, other carelessly.

Is this statement fact, opinion, or reasoned judgment? Explain why.

_____

_____

_____

_____

_____

5 Explain three specific claims by the author that suggest that the Beale pamphlet was a fake.

_____

_____

_____

_____

_____

Comparing and Contrasting

RL.7.9, RI.7.9, RH.7.9

Vocabulary
boon
stocks
truant
wantonly

What's your favorite genre to read? **Genre** is a word that means a particular kind or style of literature.

Science fiction and **fantasy** are example of genres that you know. Science-fiction stories take place in an unreal setting, such as another planet or a future Earth, or involve unreal events and nonhuman characters, but with an element of science fact as part of the background to the narrative. A fantasy, by contrast, may feature imaginary worlds, people with extraordinary powers, or fantastic creatures such as dragons or werewolves.

Books in a particular genre have elements that are similar to one another, but there is a lot of variety, too. Consider for example Nancy Farmer's *The House of the Scorpion* and Mary Logue's *Dancing with an Alien.* They are both science fiction with young people as the main characters. One is set in a scary future Earth with a boy as the main character, while the other involves a girl in love with an alien. A reader who enjoys science fiction might like them both. Or, he might care for one but not the other because of the theme or the author's style.

Realistic fiction is probably what you read most often. It is usually about people who could be real—characters who would be familiar to you—that face the same situations that modern people face.

Historical fiction can also be realistic, but it takes place in a different time. The characters in historical fiction are facing similar challenges to those in realistic fiction, but in a very different setting—ancient Egypt or America during the Civil War, for example.

When you're reading a story that involves danger, a crime, a puzzle, and a detective, you can identify it immediately as a **mystery.**

Traditional literature includes several genres of stories that people have told since before writing was invented. A **myth** may try to explain something about nature or a people's customs or beliefs. Some of the best-known myths are those of the ancient Greeks and Romans. A **legend,** like the stories of King Arthur, is a tale from the past about people and events. It is usually connected to a particular time or place. A **folktale** is a story of ordinary people that contains a lesson about human behavior. A **fable** is a very short folktale in which the characters may be animals portrayed as human types. A **fairy tale** is a kind of traditional story that involves magical creatures, interacting with human beings in good and wicked ways.

Any kind of narrative may be identified as belonging to a literary genre, even some forms of nonfiction. A **biography,** for example, is a narrative of a person's life. A **personal essay** describes and reflects upon something important to the author's life.

When you recognize the genre, you can understand better where an author is taking you and how he means for you to enjoy his work. Different genres can treat the same topics or themes in entirely different ways. A commentary on a current political issue may be disguised as fantasy or expressed as a metaphor in a poem. Historical fiction can spin a story around real events and people. It can make use of, or even change, what actually happened in the interest of telling a good story.

Review the passage, "The Web of Trade" on pages 118–119 before reading the next passage. Use what you read in *both* passages to answer the questions.

Guided Practice

Read the story. Then answer the questions.

from **Forty Days at Gao**

by Jonas Houston

"Stick close by me," Uncle Guy said. "If anyone addresses you in Arabic, answer him in French."

Dutifully Bernard answered in French. "Why should I pretend I don't know their tongue?" he asked.

"All right then, don't believe me," Uncle Guy said. "Go ahead, see what it'll get you."

"But I thought it would be a mark of respect to speak their language."

"It's not their language," Uncle Guy said. They had come to a dead stop. A caravan of heavily laden camels was blocking their path, prodded by half a dozen cursing camel drivers. Bernard thought he recognized one from the inn at Sijilmasa. But that was 50 days ago, 50 days across that demon-haunted desert. Watching the beasts' wallowing gait almost made him sick again, and he shut his eyes.

Uncle Guy took advantage of the interruption. "Every province in Songhai speaks a different tongue," he explained. "Every village, almost. In our world, priests and learned men all know Latin so that a Frenchman may speak with an Italian or a German. Among the Saracens and Moors, Arabic is the language of learning, and of trade, too. That's why everyone spoke it on the journey. Nobody will mistake me for a Moor with my fair skin. But if they hear you speaking Arabic, they may well take you for a truant schoolboy."

"Would they beat me?" He had never envied his friends in Carcassonne who had to sit in school all day and were beaten for being slow.

> This story takes place in the year 1352. Bernard's parents have recently died. Use the Internet to find out what event had just taken place in Europe. How do you think Bernard's parents died?

> **truant**
> *staying away from school*

"Worse, lad. They'll chain you in the market and make you recite the Koran."

"But I don't know the Koran!"

"So much the worse for you then." Uncle Guy cuffed him and smiled. "I'm jesting, lad. Not about the chain—it's like being put in the stocks back home, to make an example of you. They'd figure out soon enough that you're a Christian and turn you loose. See, your mother's people prize learning above all else. It's a disgrace if a man hasn't memorized all their laws and commentaries. You'll see for yourself. The trade in salt and cloth is frantic, but the trade in books is like nothing you can imagine."

stocks
a heavy wooden frame with holes for hands and feet, used as punishment

They had resumed their walk through the crowded street. It was barely wide enough to pass an ox-cart. Uncle Guy pushed his slow-hasty way past merchants, customers, slaves, gamesters, men in flowing white robes, and women in brightly colored European cloth. Some of them looked sharply at Uncle Guy, so obviously a foreigner despite his native dress, but they hardly spared Bernard a glance.

A boy of 8 or 9 sprang up before them. He juggled four bronze rings while he balanced a fifth on his nose. Bernard laughed appreciatively. "Keep your hand on your purse," Uncle Guy said in French. "Such children are often decoys for thieves." He said something to the boy that Bernard didn't catch and tossed him a copper coin.

So this was Gao, the city of gold—except it seemed made of red earth, as if the desert itself had birthed it. Even the smells were foreign! It was plain from the beggars he saw that everyone was *not* a rich merchant, but his mother had spoken truly when she told him Gao had no city wall. This is her world, Bernard thought. The song she had often sung to him was in his mind, and—no, he could hear it! Someone was playing it on a stringed instrument! The very same melody! Bernard looked around for the musician, but just then the press of the crowd suddenly eased, and he and his uncle were thrust into the great marketplace like a river bursting into the sea.

"Do your gawking later," Uncle Guy said with a sharp dig of his elbow. "Let's go find Ali and our goods and see if we can do some business."

The setting of this historical fiction is ____.

A China

B Egypt

C East Africa

D West Africa

Rereading "The Web of Trade" before reading this excerpt refreshes your memory of some of the place names. Bernard and his uncle have crossed the desert from Sijilmasa to Gao. You know from the article that this was a common trade route in West Africa, and the map illustrating the article shows you exactly where Bernard and Uncle Guy are. The correct answer is choice D.

Explain how the author has departed from true history in telling his story.

A The riches of Gao were nothing more than a legend.

B The French and the West Africans were actually at war.

C More usually it was African traders, not Europeans, who crossed the Sahara Desert.

D European traders in West Africa at the time would have kept their true origin hidden.

Historical fiction writers will sometimes set real events aside to tell a story. The gold of West Africa was no legend, and there was no fighting then between Europeans and Africans, and no reason for either to hide their origin from each other. However, the article suggests that the cross-desert trade was carried on by Africans, and it was only the most adventurous European who ventured to West Africa—like the trader mentioned in the article who married the African princess. On that story, maybe the author based the idea of Bernard born in France of an African mother. Choice C is the correct answer.

Analyze the story. What facts and themes in the article "The Web of Trade"
are reflected in this story?

_____

_____

_____

_____

_____

✓ Authors of historical fiction will depart from actual details, but they had
better stick close to the most important facts or they're writing fantasy. Here
is a sample answer:

> The historical background to this story is Africa as a center of
> trade from the 13th through the 15th centuries. The setting is the
> city of Gao, which grew fabulously rich on the trade in gold. It was
> exchanged for cloth and metal goods from Europe, which is probably
> what Bernard and his uncle have brought across the desert.

What are two details in this story that are *not* in the nonfiction article?

_____

_____

_____

_____

✓ A historian is usually concerned with broad themes and the facts that
illuminate them. "The Web of Trade" has details on trade routes and what
goods were bought and sold where, but it doesn't tell you much about
what you'd see in a West African market. That is where a fiction writer's
imagination comes into play. Here is a sample answer:

> A child caught ditching school would be chained in the marketplace
> and made to recite religious verses as punishment. There were
> jugglers and musicians to entertain the people buying and selling,
> and maybe to distract them while thieves stole their money.

Comparing and Contrasting Informational Texts ——

In informational text, too, authors tell stories in different ways. Two authors writing on the same topic will emphasize different evidence or interpret facts differently. A key event in a person's life will be reported and interpreted differently in a news article about her than in a biography written by a person who knew her. A biography written long after the subject is dead will have yet a different approach to her story. Likewise, a soldier's firsthand account of a battle will have a different perspective than a historian's account written after the war is over. By comparing and contrasting such sources, you are often able to combine facts in a way that gives you a better perspective on what really happened.

Review the passage, "Marching Through Georgia" on pages 147–149 before reading the next passage. Use what you read in both passages to answer the questions.

Guided Practice

Read the passage. Then answer the questions.

from **The War-Time Journal of a Georgia Girl**

by Eliza Frances Andrews

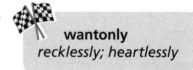

You can read Eliza Frances Andrews's complete Civil War diary on the Internet.

December 24, 1864

About three miles from Sparta we struck the "Burnt Country," as it is well named by the natives, and then I could better understand the wrath and desperation of these poor people. I almost felt as if I should like to hang a Yankee myself. There was hardly a fence left standing all the way from Sparta to Gordon. The fields were trampled down and the road was lined with carcasses of horses, hogs, and cattle that the invaders, unable either to consume or to carry away with them, had wantonly shot down to starve out the people and prevent them from making their crops. The stench in some places was unbearable; every few hundred yards we had to hold our noses or stop them with the cologne Mrs. Elzey had given us, and it proved a great boon. The dwellings that were standing all showed signs of pillage, and on every plantation we saw the charred remains of the gin-house and packing-screw, while here and there, lone chimney-stacks, "Sherman's Sentinels," told of homes laid in ashes. The infamous wretches! I couldn't wonder now that these poor people should want to put a rope round the neck of every red-handed "devil of them" they could lay their hands on. Hay ricks and fodder stacks were demolished, corn cribs were empty, and every bale of cotton that could be found was burnt by the savages. I saw no grain of any sort, except little patches they had spilled when feeding their horses and which there was not even a chicken left in the country to eat. A bag of oats might have lain anywhere along the road without danger from the beasts of the field,

wantonly
recklessly; heartlessly

boon
favor; kindness

UNIT 4 ░░
Integration of Knowledge and Ideas

though I cannot say it would have been safe from the assaults of hungry man. Crowds of soldiers were tramping over the road in both directions; it was like traveling through the streets of a populous town all day. They were mostly on foot, and I saw numbers seated on the roadside greedily eating raw turnips, meat skins, parched corn—anything they could find, even picking up the loose grains that Sherman's horses had left. I felt tempted to stop and empty the contents of our provision baskets into their laps, but the dreadful accounts that were given of the state of the country before us, made prudence get the better of our generosity....

Before crossing the Oconee at Milledgeville we ascended an immense hill, from which there was a fine view of the town, with Gov. Brown's fortifications in the foreground and the river rolling at our feet. The Yankees had burnt the bridge, so we had to cross on a ferry. There was a long train of vehicles ahead of us, and it was nearly an hour before our turn came, so we had ample time to look about us. On our left was a field where 30,000 Yankees had camped hardly three weeks before. It was strewn with the *débris* they had left behind, and the poor people of the neighborhood were wandering over it, seeking for anything they could find to eat, even picking up grains of corn that were scattered around where the Yankees had fed their horses. We were told that a great many valuables were found there at first, plunder that the invaders had left behind, but the place had been picked over so often by this time that little now remained except tufts of loose cotton, piles of half-rotted grain, and the carcasses of slaughtered animals, which raised a horrible stench. Some men were plowing in one part of the field, making ready for next year's crop.

Compare this diary entry and the article on pages 147–149. What is most similar between them?

_____

_____

_____

Eliza Frances Andrews (1840–1931) was a well-known Southern writer in her day. Both her diary entry and Paul Williams's article are describing the same event. Here is a sample answer:

Both are concerned with Sherman's march through Georgia, the destruction brought about by Sherman's army, and the hardships people faced as a result.

Determine which of these themes or topics is *not* discussed in Andrews's entry?

A   Sherman's military strategy

B   Sherman's tactic of "total war"

C   The anger of the people of Georgia

D   Burned bridges hampering people's efforts to escape

Andrews is not concerned with war plans or the way an army is organized. She describes the results of Sherman's march, both in general terms and in detail, and the reaction of the people in his way, but she couldn't care less about his strategy. Choice A is the correct answer.

How does the difference in narrative voice influence the tone of the two accounts and the way events are described?

_____

_____

_____

_____

_____

_____

_____

✓ Paul Williams's secondary-source account, written nearly 150 years after the events it describes, summarizes the march and its effects. Eliza Andrews, by contrast, was there, and she describes what she saw and experienced. Here is a sample answer:

Williams's third-person account makes use of several diaries like Andrews's, both from Northern soldiers and from the Southern people who were in their way, as well as army records. He mostly describes what happened, from the perspective of all his sources and his own point of view. Andrews's is a primary source. She describes the destruction, but with personal details of what she saw, like people picking through the dirt for food to eat, chimneys being all that are left of the houses, and the stench of dead animals. You get her sense of outrage and despair when she talks about how she's ready to hang a Yankee.

How might a historical novelist use the material in both accounts?

_____

_____

_____

_____

✓ A novelist might stick with actual events or ask "What if" and imagine a story only loosely based on the events. There are many ways to answer the question. Here is a sample answer:

A novelist could make up a character based on a Union soldier on the march and another based on a Southern woman like Eliza Andrews and have them meet, interact, and have their thoughts and feelings changed by the experience.

UNIT 4
Integration of Knowledge and Ideas

Test Yourself

Read the passage and review the two scenes from the play *For the Crime of Voting* on pages 73–75 and 103–104. Then answer the questions.

On Women's Right to Vote

by Susan B. Anthony

Susan B. Anthony

Susan Brownell Anthony (1820–1906) was arrested for voting in the 1872 presidential election. She grew up in a liberal Quaker family in Massachusetts. As a young unmarried woman, she became personally aware of how women were disadvantaged by their lack of personal and economic freedom. She was also involved in the movements for temperance and the abolition of slavery and was devoted to those causes. At a temperance meeting in 1852, when she stood to speak, Lewis Tappan, who was chairing the meeting, ordered her to sit down. Tappan, who had risked his fortune and his personal safety in the Abolitionist cause, said to her, "The sisters were not invited here to speak but to listen and learn." Anthony stormed out of the building. She devoted the rest of her long life to the cause of equal rights for women.

In 1873, while awaiting her trial for voting, Anthony toured New York State giving variations on the speech excerpted below. At her trial, she was found guilty of the crime of voting without having the lawful right to vote and was fined $100. "I will never pay a dollar," she said, and she never did.

I stand before you under indictment for the alleged crime of having voted at the last presidential election, without having a lawful right to vote. It shall be my work this evening to prove to you that in thus doing, I not only committed no crime, but instead simply exercised my citizen's rights, guaranteed to me and all United States citizens by the… Constitution beyond the power of any state to deny.

Our democratic-republican government is based on the idea of the natural right of every individual member thereof to a voice and a vote…. We throw to the winds the old dogma that government can give rights. No one denies that before governments were organized, each individual possessed the right to protect his own life, liberty, and property. When…people enter into a free government, they do not barter away their natural rights…. The Declaration of Independence [and] the United States Constitution…propose to protect the people in the exercise of their God-given rights.

"All men are created equal and endowed by their creator with certain inalienable rights…. To secure these, governments are instituted among men, deriving their just powers from the consent of the governed." Here is no shadow of government authority over rights, or exclusion of any class from their full and equal enjoyment. Here is pronounced the rights of all men, and consequently…of all women, to a voice in the government. And here, in the first paragraph of the Declaration, is the assertion of the natural right to all of the ballot; for how can "the consent of the governed" be given if the right to vote be denied?... The women, dissatisfied as they are with this form of government, that enforces taxation without representation—that compels them to obey laws to which they have never given their consent—that robs them, in marriage, of the custody of their own persons, wages, and children—are this half of the people who are left wholly at the mercy of the other half, in direct violation of…the declarations of the framers of this government, every one of which was based on the immutable principle of equal rights to all.…

The Preamble of the Federal Constitution says: "We, the people of the United States"… not we, the white male citizens, nor we, the male citizens, but we, the whole people, who formed this union. We formed it not to give the blessings of liberty but to secure them; not to the half of ourselves and the half of our posterity, but to the whole people— women as well as men. It is downright mockery to talk to women of their enjoyment of the blessings of liberty while they are denied the only means of securing them provided by this… government—the ballot.…

1 In both the play and in her speech, Anthony _____.

   A refers to her family life

   B quotes the Constitution

   C expresses her resolve to go to jail

   D speaks of the right to vote as a "natural right"

2 Determine which of these lines from the play is explained in greater detail in the introduction to the speech.

   A I want my arrest to be as public as possible.

   B I will sue each of you personally for large, exemplary damages!

   C I have been silenced in temperance meetings and in abolition meetings.

   D You may not know how many women are regularly beaten by their husbands.

3 In her play, how does Jan Kelter have Anthony express the views that Anthony herself expressed in her speech?

_____

_____

_____

_____

_____

4 How does the introduction to Anthony's speech provide information that helps explain the content of the speech?

_____

_____

_____

_____

_____

5 Based on information in the introduction and the speech, what are some likely reasons that Anthony undertook the speaking tour? Explain why.

_____

_____

_____

_____

_____

6 Which of these details in the play was *most likely* not based on history but made up by Jan Kelter?

    A Susan B. Anthony's three sisters

    B Judge Selden having known Anthony's father

    C the conversation among the men in the barbershop

    D Judge Selden being troubled by the possibility of Susan's going to jail

7 Explain your answer to question 6.

_____

_____

_____

_____

_____

8 Based on information in the speech and the introduction, what will happen in later scenes of Kelter's play?

_____

_____

_____

_____

_____

UNIT 4 ▨▨
Integration of Knowledge and Ideas

REVIEW

Integration of Knowledge and Ideas

UNIT

4

Vocabulary
Cossack
flanks
league
skirmish

Read the poem and the essay. Then answer the questions.

The Charge of the Light Brigade

by Alfred, Lord Tennyson

Written in 1854, this poem commemorates an incident in the Crimean War, in which Britain was fighting against Russia.

Half a league[1], half a league,
Half a league onward,
All in the valley of Death
Rode the six hundred.
5 "Forward, the Light Brigade!
Charge for the guns!" he said:
Into the valley of Death
Rode the six hundred.

"Forward, the Light Brigade!"
10 Was there a man dismayed?
Not though the soldier knew
Some one had blundered:
Theirs not to make reply,
Theirs not to reason why,
15 Theirs but to do and die:
Into the valley of Death
Rode the six hundred.

[1]**league:** measurement of distance

Cannon to right of them,
Cannon to left of them,
20 Cannon in front of them
Volleyed and thundered;
Stormed at with shot and shell,
Boldly they rode and well,
Into the jaws of Death,
25 Into the mouth of Hell
Rode the six hundred.

Flashed all their sabers bare,
Flashed as they turned in air
Sabring the gunners there,
30 Charging an army, while
All the world wondered:
Plunged in the battery-smoke
Right through the line they broke;
Cossack[2] and Russian
35 Reeled from the saber-stroke
Shattered and sundered.
Then they rode back, but not
Not the six hundred.

Cannon to right of them,
40 Cannon to left of them,
Cannon behind them
Volleyed and thundered;
Stormed at with shot and shell,
While horse and hero fell,
45 They that had fought so well
Came through the jaws of Death,
Back from the mouth of Hell,
All that was left of them,
Left of six hundred.

50 When can their glory fade?
O the wild charge they made!
All the world wondered.
Honor the charge they made!
Honor the Light Brigade,
55 Noble six hundred.

---

[2]**Cossack:** cavalry soldiers from the Ukraine and southern Russia

Down in the Valley of Death

by Richard Henry

The Battle of Balaclava would be a forgotten skirmish in a forgotten war were it not for a disastrous charge made by a small British cavalry unit against the Russians. "The charge of the light brigade" was memorialized in a famous poem by Alfred Lord Tennyson, England's Poet Laureate. The story was later retold, with varying degrees of accuracy, in a novel and two Hollywood movies. Net surfers can access a scratchy 1890 recording of the poem as declaimed by Tennyson himself.

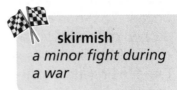

skirmish
a minor fight during a war

What makes this tale of soldiers on horseback compelling in the age of drone strikes and suicide bombers? It's because Tennyson's poem captures war both in the romantic way some like to think of it and in its horrifying reality. The poet deftly walks a tightrope between patriotism and frank criticism of his country's military leaders. "The Charge of the Light Brigade" is a story of the bravery of soldiers and the vanity and stupidity of their officers.

This was the situation at Balaclava on the afternoon of October 24, 1854: The "light brigade," consisting of between 600 and 670 men, was commanded by Major General the Earl of Cardigan. His commanding officer was Lieutenant General the Earl of Lucan. The two men were brothers-in law and had hated each other for 30 years. The Russians occupied the high ground on both sides of a valley, Causeway Heights to the right of the British cavalry and the Fedioukine Hills to the left. They had just captured two British forts on the far side of Causeway Heights. Lucan could not see them from down in the valley, but British army commander Lord Raglan was situated on higher ground to the west, where he could. He wanted to stop the Russians from taking the cannon from these forts. He sent Captain Lewis Nolan with a message to Lucan for the cavalry to "advance rapidly to the front, follow the enemy, and try to prevent the enemy from carrying away the guns." Nolan further indicated that Lucan was to attack immediately. When Lucan asked which guns were meant, Nolan is said to have gestured with a sweep of his arm, apparently indicating a fort at the far end of the valley, about a mile away.

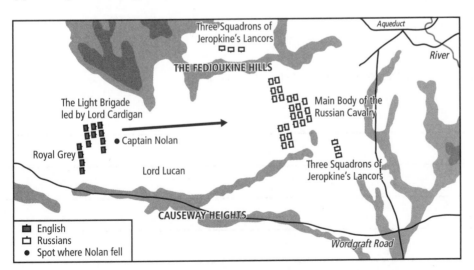

Lucan ordered Cardigan to lead the "light brigade" straight into the valley toward that fort. Lucan himself was to follow with the "heavy brigade." As soon as Captain Nolan saw Cardigan begin the charge, he dashed out on his horse in front of Cardigan. It is thought that Nolan realized Cardigan was going after the wrong target and was trying to turn the brigade, but he was hit by a Russian artillery shell and killed instantly. It was the first of many British deaths. Cannon fire fell on the light brigade from three sides. They were able to force the Russians out of the fort but were quickly pushed back under withering fire.

Lucan did not send his troops in support but remained at the head of the valley. Later, he would explain that he saw no point in having a second brigade slaughtered, and that he was in the best position to aid survivors of the charge as they returned. It was believed by many, though, that he was motivated by his hatred for his brother-in-law. Cardigan, meanwhile, charged bravely at the head of his troops, but returned alone, not bothering to find out what had happened to the survivors. He would explain that he was so angry at Nolan, who he had thought was trying to take command of the charge from him, that he wasn't thinking clearly. While the battle was still raging, he left for his yacht in Balaclava Harbor and ate a fancy dinner.

Of the "noble 600," 178 men were killed or taken prisoner, and 127 more were wounded. For the rest of their lives, Lucan and Cardigan would blame each other for the disaster. Tennyson's poem would turn the charge into a symbol of courage and tragedy. But a French general who was present at the battle would say it better than the poet: "It is magnificent, but it is not war. It is madness."

1 Identify which aspect of the battle is illustrated by the painting by Richard Caton Woodville, shown on page 181.

   A Lord Lucan's mistake

   B the futility of the charge

   C the bravery of the British soldiers

   D the placement of the Russian guns

2 Explain how the map on page 183 helps your understanding of both the essay *and* the poem.

_____

_____

_____

_____

_____

UNIT 4 ✖✖✖
Integration of Knowledge and Ideas

3 How does the essay explain what Tennyson means in lines 5 and 6 of the poem? How does it explain line 12?

_____

_____

_____

_____

_____

4 Determine which of these sentences from the first paragraph of the essay states an opinion.

   A The Battle of Balaclava would be a forgotten skirmish in a forgotten war were it not for a disastrous charge made by a small British cavalry unit against the Russians.

   B "The charge of the light brigade" was memorialized in a famous poem by Alfred Lord Tennyson, England's Poet Laureate.

   C The story was later retold, with varying degrees of accuracy, in a novel and two Hollywood movies.

   D Net surfers can access a scratchy 1890 recording of the poem as declaimed by Tennyson himself.

5 Richard Henry writes that Tennyson "walks a tightrope between patriotism and frank criticism of his country's military leaders." Does the poem offer evidence of this statement? Explain why, or why not.

_____

_____

_____

_____

_____

6 Henry blames the disaster on the "vanity and stupidity of their officers." Is this claim based on sound evidence? Explain why, or why not.

_____

_____

_____

_____

_____

7 Read this statement from the passage.

> Cardigan...returned alone, not bothering to find out what had happened to the survivors.

Is this statement fact, opinion, or reasoned judgment? Explain why.

_____

_____

_____

_____

_____

Read the passage. Then answer the questions.

Lord Cardigan gave the following account of "the charge of the light brigade" at a banquet in London a few months after the Battle of Balaclava:

We advanced down a gradual descent of more than three-quarters of a mile, with the batteries vomiting forth upon us shells and shot… with one battery [of cannon] on our right flank and another on the left, and all the intermediate ground covered with the Russian riflemen; so that when we came to within a distance of fifty yards from the mouths of the artillery which had been hurling destruction upon us, we were, in fact, surrounded and encircled by a blaze of fire, in addition to the fire of the riflemen upon our flanks.

As we ascended the hill, the oblique fire of the artillery poured upon our rear, so that we had thus a strong fire upon our front, our flank, and our rear. We…went through the battery—the two leading regiments cutting down a great number of the Russian gunners in their onset. In the two regiments which I had the honor to lead, every officer, with one exception, was either killed or wounded, or had his horse shot under him or injured. Those regiments proceeded, followed by

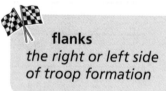
flanks
the right or left side of troop formation

UNIT 4 ▨▨▨▨▨▨▨▨▨▨▨▨▨▨▨▨▨▨▨▨▨▨▨▨▨▨▨▨▨▨▨▨
Integration of Knowledge and Ideas

the second line, consisting of two more regiments of cavalry, which continued to perform the duty of cutting down the Russian gunners.

Then came the third line…which endeavored to complete the duty assigned to our brigade. I believe that this was achieved with great success, and the result was that this body, composed of only about 670 men, succeeded in passing through the mass of Russian cavalry of—as we have since learned—5,240 strong; and having broken through that mass, they…retired in the same manner, doing as much execution in their course as they possibly could upon the enemy's cavalry. Upon our returning up the hill which we had descended in the attack, we had to run the same gauntlet and to incur the same risk from the flank fire of the [riflemen] as we had encountered before. Numbers of our men were shot down….

But what, my Lord, was the feeling and what the bearing of those brave men who returned to the position. Of each of these regiments there returned but a small detachment, two-thirds of the men engaged having been destroyed? I think that every man who was engaged in that disastrous affair at Balaklava, and who was fortunate enough to come out of it alive, must feel that it was only by a merciful decree of Almighty Providence that he escaped from the greatest apparent certainty of death which could possibly be conceived.

8 Which of these details that Cardigan mentions is not cited in Henry's essay?

    A   the number of men in his brigade

    B   the heavy losses his brigade suffered

    C   the number of enemy soldiers they faced

    D   the fire that fell on his men from every direction

9 Which of these details in Henry's essay is *also* mentioned in Cardigan's account?

    A   Nolan's trying to turn the brigade

    B   Cardigan leading the brigade into battle himself

    C   Cardigan's leaving the field before the battle was over

    D   Lucan's declining to ride into the valley in Cardigan's support

10 What are the two *main* differences between Cardigan's and Henry's interpretations of the battle? Give details to explain your answer.

_____

_____

_____

_____

_____

11 How does the painting by William Simpson on page 187 illustrate Cardigan's account of the battle? Contrast it with the painting on page 181 illustrating the poem.

_____

_____

_____

_____

_____

UNIT 4 ▨▨
Integration of Knowledge and Ideas

PRACTICE TEST

Read the poem. Then answer the questions.

To J.G., Who Sat Next to Me in Seventh-Grade Math

by Marcia Roche-Tombée

That day you brushed the spider from my purse,
Between the bike rack and the soccer field,
My terror palpable, my crush concealed
(And never could have told you which was worse)—
5 You saw me cower, helpless in my fright,
Banished Arachne with a gentle hand
To scuttle homeward down a silken strand—
I kissed you then, my square Round-Table knight!

I've seen Montmartre[1] and the Taj Mahal,
10 I heard the Beatles play Shea Stadium;
I've had a beach wedding and a church wedding,
Raced bikes up mountains, swum with sharks and stingrays in Tahiti,
    taught a class at Harvard, earned a black belt in aikido, interviewed
    a president and the Dalai Lama, gritted through days when the
    bear ate me, gloried in days when I ate the bear—

But never a prouder or more wondrous day
Than when you brushed the spider from my purse!

1 Which of these *best* describes the theme of the poem?

  A getting over one's fears

  B remembering special moments

  C recognizing how one has changed

  D reconnecting with a long-lost friend

---

[1]**Montmartre:** a famous district in Paris, France

2 From its relation to the word *concealed,* you can tell that <u>palpable</u> in line 3 means _____.

    A false

    B foolish

    C obvious

    D unimportant

3 The speaker's calling the boy her "square Round-Table knight" (line 8) is an allusion to _____.

    A the legend of King Arthur

    B a character from a famous poem

    C a historical figure of the 15th century

    D a myth about an ancient Greek hero

4 What does the poet mean by the metaphor about the bear in line 12?

    A A person will eat anything if she's hungry enough.

    B It's a tough world, and you have to be strong to survive.

    C There are days when you feel like a loser and days when you feel like a winner.

    D If you're afraid of spiders, how would you feel about something really dangerous?

5 In the poem, how can you tell that the speaker is laughing at herself for having once been afraid of spiders?

_____

_____

_____

_____

_____

6 Explain in a summary how the poet develops her theme over the course of the poem.

_____

_____

_____

_____

_____

7 How does the repetition of sounds in lines 1–8 and in lines 9 and 11 affect your reading of the poem?

_____

_____

_____

_____

_____

8 How does the poet use the sonnet form to add meaning to her poem?

_____

_____

_____

_____

_____

Man's Best Friend—for 30,000 Years?

by Andrew Paltz

Goyet Cave in Belgium is one of the world's most famous Stone Age sites. Discovered in the 19th century, it has long yielded data about Paleolithic humans, the animals they ate, and the cave bears that sometimes ate them. In 2008, the cave revealed a new surprise. A fossil skull, dated to about 31,700 years ago, is thought to be the remains of the earliest known domestic dog.

It was a well-established hypothesis that the partnership between dogs and humans was what separated dogs from their ancestors, the gray wolves. The unanswered questions for science were just when and where the divergence into different species began, and what humans, rather than nature, had to do with it. Dogs and dog fossils differ in several ways from modern and prehistoric wolves. The dog's snout is shorter and wider, suggesting an animal that was fed more by humans than by hunting. The skull is significantly shorter, while the brain case is wider. By these criteria, the animal found in Goyet Cave is decidedly dog, not wolf.

Wolf

Dog

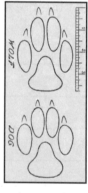

Paw Prints

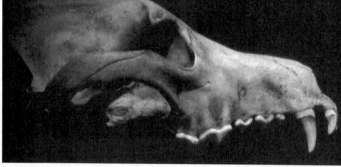

Wolf Skull

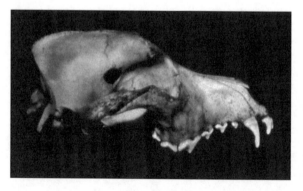

Dog Skull

The finding poses to science its most frequent challenge: whether to question an accepted hypothesis based on new data, or whether to question the data. There had once been general agreement that the dog was domesticated around 14,000 years ago, and that it happened in China. That *determination* was based on analysis of canine DNA, which suggested that modern dogs had a common ancestor around that place and time. It was assumed that humans and wolves formed a kind of partnership, by which people got help with hunting and herding, and wolves got shelter and a reliable food source. Humans selectively bred the wolves that they tamed, and in time the two species diverged.

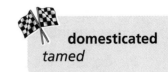

domesticated
tamed

The Goyet Cave dog is only the most recent piece of evidence to challenge that hypothesis. A more recent study of dog DNA, which used more data than the earlier study, suggests that dogs and wolves began to separate as species about 100,000 years ago. While dog bones don't show up in the fossil record until much later, there are fossil wolf bones found with the remains of humans from much longer than 100,000 years ago. Another DNA study indicated that dogs have more genes in common with wild wolves in the Middle East than those in China. Before the Goyet discovery, the earliest fossils that were unquestionably dog date to around 14,000 years ago, and they are found buried at the same sites as human fossils—sometimes, as in a site in Germany, in the same grave.

So what is science to make of the Goyet Cave dog? It looked like a dog. It was associated with humans. Chemical analysis of its cells showed that it ate a diet rich in reindeer, horse, and musk ox. These animals are too large usually to be hunted by wolves, but were certainly hunted by Stone-Age humans and could have been fed to dogs. Yet if dogs were domesticated 31,700 years ago, why is there a gap in the fossil record for the next 17,700 years? Might the Goyet dog be a more recent animal whose bones got mixed up with older human fossils (a problem that often confounds archaeologists and paleontologists)? Could it actually have been a wolf with an oddly shaped skull caused by its diet? Or was it a transitional animal, no longer quite wolf but not yet a dog?

And what do the recent discoveries suggest about when and how the dog was domesticated? Could the dog have been domesticated independently by several groups of humans, far apart in place and time? Might the dog actually have begun the process 100,000 years ago by choosing for its own survival "reasons" to associate with humans? Might changes in human culture 14,000 years ago have led to changes in the ways they used dogs, and so to changes in the traits that they bred for? Among all these questions, one idea remains constant: If the dog is not "man's best friend" among the animals, it is certainly our oldest.

9 The author of this article *mainly* wants to ____.

    A express his feelings about the close relationship between dogs and humans

    B explain new evidence that challenges older ideas about when the dog was domesticated

    C persuade readers that science changes its views so often that it can't be taken seriously

    D show that dogs and humans have been partners for much longer than was previously believed

10 The photos and illustrations on page 192 are meant to demonstrate ____.

    A how dogs and wolves diverged from a common ancestor

    B how scientists can distinguish between dog and wolf fossils

    C why it is so hard to determine exactly when dogs were domesticated

    D why scientists can't agree whether the fossil skull found in the Goyet Cave is from a dog or a wolf

11 According to the author, what evidence *best* indicates that the fossil from the Goyet Cave is a dog and not a wolf skull?

_____

_____

_____

_____

_____

12 How does the information in paragraph 3 fit into the overall structure of the passage and contribute to its ideas?

_____

_____

_____

_____

_____

13 As used in paragraph 3, the word <u>determination</u> means _____.

   A the act of deciding

   B the state of being decided

   C great firmness in carrying out a purpose

   D finding out exactly by weighing, measuring, or calculating

14 As used in biology, what does the word <u>divergence</u> mean (paragraph 2)?

_____

_____

_____

_____

_____

15 According to the article, the dog and wolf began to separate into different species long before the dog became domesticated. What evidence does the author cite? Is it sufficient to support his claim? Is his reasoning sound? Explain why, or why not.

_____

_____

_____

_____

_____

16 In the last paragraph, the author suggests that dogs, not humans, may have begun the domestication process to improve their chances for survival. Is this a fact, reasoned judgment, or pure speculation on the author's part? Explain why.

_____

_____

_____

_____

_____

from **Roughing It**

by Mark Twain

In 1860, before he adopted his famous pen name, Samuel L. Clemens traveled by stagecoach from Missouri to Nevada and on to California. Thirty years later, he published the story of his adventures, probably not without embellishment.

In a little while all interest was taken up in stretching our necks and watching for the "pony-rider"—the fleet messenger who sped across the continent from St. Joe to Sacramento, carrying letters nineteen hundred miles in eight days! Think of that for perishable horse and human flesh and blood to do! The pony-rider was usually a little bit of a man, brimful of spirit and endurance. No matter what time of the day or night his watch came on, and no matter whether it was winter or summer, raining, snowing, hailing, or sleeting, or whether his "beat" was a level straight road or a crazy trail over mountain crags and precipices, or whether it led through peaceful regions or regions that swarmed with hostile Indians, he must be always ready to leap into the saddle and be off like the wind! There was no idling-time for a pony-rider on duty. He rode fifty miles without stopping, by daylight, moonlight, starlight, or through the blackness of darkness—just as it happened. He rode a splendid horse that was born for a racer and fed and lodged like a gentleman; kept him at his utmost speed for ten miles, and then, as he came crashing up to the station where stood two men holding fast a fresh, impatient steed, the transfer of rider and mail-bag was made in the twinkling of an eye, and away flew the eager pair and were out of sight before the spectator could get hardly the ghost of a look. Both rider and horse went "flying light." The rider's dress was thin, and fitted close; he wore a "round-about," and a skull-cap, and tucked his pantaloons into his boot-tops like a race-rider. He carried no arms—he carried nothing that was not absolutely necessary, for even the postage on his literary freight was worth *five dollars a letter.*

He got but little frivolous correspondence to carry—his bag had business letters in it, mostly. His horse was stripped of all unnecessary weight, too. He wore a little wafer of a racing-saddle, and no visible blanket. He wore light shoes, or none at all. The little flat mail-pockets strapped under the rider's thighs would each hold about the bulk of a child's primer. They held many and many an important business chapter and newspaper letter, but these were written on paper as airy and thin as gold leaf, nearly, and thus bulk and weight were economized. The stagecoach traveled about a hundred to a hundred and twenty-five miles a day (twenty-four hours), the pony-rider about two hundred and fifty. There were about eighty pony-riders in the saddle all the time, night and day, stretching in a long, scattering procession from Missouri to California, forty flying eastward, and forty toward the west, and among them making four hundred gallant horses earn a stirring livelihood and see a deal of scenery every single day in the year.

We had had a consuming desire, from the beginning, to see a pony-rider, but somehow or other all that passed us and all that met us managed to streak by in the night, and so we heard only a whiz and a hail, and the swift phantom of the desert was gone before we could get our heads out of the windows. But now we were expecting one along every moment, and would see him in broad daylight. Presently the driver exclaims:

"HERE HE COMES!"

Every neck is stretched further, and every eye strained wider. Away across the endless dead level of the prairie a black speck appears against the sky, and it is plain that it moves. Well, I should think so!

In a second or two it becomes a horse and rider, rising and falling, rising and falling—sweeping toward us nearer and nearer—growing more and more distinct, more and more sharply defined—nearer and still nearer, and the flutter of the hoofs comes faintly to the ear—another instant a whoop and a hurrah from our upper deck, a wave of the rider's hand, but no reply, and man and horse burst past our excited faces, and go winging away like a belated fragment of a storm!

So sudden is it all, and so like a flash of unreal fancy, that but for the flake of white foam left quivering and perishing on a mail-sack after the vision had flashed by and disappeared, we might have doubted whether we had seen any actual horse and man at all, maybe.

17 The word <u>steed</u>, as a synonym for *horse,* connotes _____.

A a fast racer

B a warhorse

C a fancy show horse

D a fine and noble horse

18 Explain how the words Twain uses to describe the Pony Express horses affect his meaning and tone.

_____

_____

_____

_____

_____

19 Analyze the passage. How do Twain as narrator, the event he describes, the setting, and the rider interact to create the tone of the excerpt?

_____

_____

_____

_____

_____

20 According to Twain, how many times did a Pony Express rider have to change horses while riding his route? Explain using evidence from the passage.

_____

_____

_____

_____

_____

21 Describe how Twain uses figurative language to emphasize how lightly the rider traveled.

_____

_____

_____

_____

_____

22 What was Twain's *main* purpose in writing this passage? What aspects of the text reveal this purpose?

_____

_____

_____

_____

_____

Read the story. Then answer the questions.

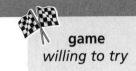

game
willing to try

from **Enos Campbell**

by Ramona Stuart

I was seated on the porch, trying to catch what breeze there was. The flag hung limply from its standard, but the air must have been moving somewhere on account of the little yellow dust devils that kept rising a foot or so from the street and disintegrating into a million motes, as if they figured what was the use. Apart from the clanking of Hiram's and Clooney's blacksmith's hammers from opposite ends of the street, the only sound was the buzzing of the flies.

That was how I first set eyes on Enos Campbell. He came riding up about as slow as the day, on the sorriest swaybacked old plowhorse you ever saw. He stopped in front of the Baptist church and stood there a minute like he was trying to decide whether to go in and say a prayer. I could tell he saw me though because he kept looking away when I caught his eye.

Finally, I raised my hat back on my forehead just a mite and said, "Something I can do for you, son?"

He shaded his eyes and squinted like he was pretending he'd just noticed me, like he wasn't desperate for a job and a ticket off the farm like a thousand other lads in the territory. Then he rode up, a little too quickly for the act he was putting on, and said, "Would you be Mr. Blanton Hicks?"

"That I am, son."

He dismounted and came up the steps to the porch, a good deal livelier than his horse. His hand was already out by the second step, and I stood to shake it.

"My name's Enos Campbell, and I hear you're looking for fast riders for this new express mail route."

I looked him up and down. He looked fit enough for the part, about five foot seven in his boots, no more than a hundred and ten pounds, as skinny and tough as a strip of beef jerky and about the same color from outdoor work.

"How old are you, Enos Campbell?"

"Seventeen, sir," he said, too quickly.

"Sure, and I'm Queen Victoria's handmaiden. The truth, son."

He flushed then, and I knew he wasn't a day over 14. "Paper in the post office said you was looking for fearless riders without no family obligations. Didn't say nothing about age."

"You ever ride anything more spirited than that jade you come in on?"

"Mr. Hicks, you put me on the fastest horse you got, and you'll see how good I can ride."

He had gumption, young Master Enos Campbell, I had to hand that to him. "Well, we'll see about that in a minute." I waved a hand at his steed. "That belong to your pa?"

"My ma. My pa lit out for California when I was yea high, lookin' for gold. I reckon he was killed by Injuns or something 'cause my ma ain't had a letter in a while."

More likely he went bust and stayed away out of shame, but I didn't say that to Enos Campbell. I knew about men and California and gold fever from personal experience.

"And you think you can help your ma out better riding Pony Express than staying on the farm?"

"She don't need my help. She's got Uncle Jake now, and he don't want me around. Anyway he ain't really my uncle."

I was beginning to get the picture. I gave the boy another look. He looked dumb enough to think he was going to ride clear to California and find his pa, but he looked game enough to actually do it.

"Come on into my office, son, and we'll talk," I said, and I saw he had the manners to wipe his boots before he came in.

The office was dark after the sunlit street, and I could see his eyes trying to get big enough to see. "Let me tell you something about the job, Campbell," I said. "I figure all you know about it is that it pays $25 cash dollars a week, a heap more than you can get from railroad work. You'll be in the saddle 75 to a 100 miles at a stretch, 10, 11 hours, day or night, summer or winter, maybe double that if another rider is incapacitated. You'll carry nothing but a water sack and a revolver besides the mail, and you're to protect the mail at all costs, even at the risk of your horse and your life. Is that clear?"

"Yes, sir!" Campbell said, straightening himself up.

"Would you be willing to swear to this agreement?" I said, pushing the paper across my desk.

He did not touch the paper but sat there staring at it. "I can't read so good," he said.

My picture of Master Enos Campbell had another piece filled in. "Well, I don't reckon you'll have much call for reading while you're in the saddle," I said. "Mr. Alexander Majors, who owns this company, is a Christian gentleman, and he expects every man to act the same. Let me read it to you." I recited from memory: "'While I am in the employ of A. Majors, I agree not to use profane language, not to get drunk, not to gamble, not to treat animals cruelly and not to do anything else that is incompatible with the conduct of a gentleman. And I agree, if I violate any of the above conditions, to accept my discharge without any pay for my services.'"

profane
vulgar, bad

"I can swear to that," Campbell said.

I looked at him a moment longer, then stood and beckoned at him. "Let's go visit the stable," I said. "Time to find out if you can ride as good as you say you can."

23 *Integer* is a Latin word that means "whole," or "together." What does the word *disintegrating* mean in paragraph 1?

_____

_____

_____

_____

_____

24 In this excerpt, how does the author establish the points of view of both Hicks and Campbell?

_____

_____

_____

_____

_____

25 What is the setting of the story, and how does it affect the characters and the events that are described?

_____

_____

_____

_____

_____

26 How does this fictional story about the Pony Express compare and contrast with Mark Twain's account in _Roughing It?_

_____

_____

_____

_____

_____

The Pony Express: A Fast, Brief Gallop

by Joseph Seay

The Pony Express was in operation for barely 19 months, from April 1860 through October 1861. As a business, it was a failure. As an event, it remains a legend to this day. What was essentially a low-tech predecessor to Fed-Ex remains part of the lore of the West, a symbol of American grit and individualism.

The Pony Express was first and foremost a business venture. It was organized by three men, William H. Russell, William B. Waddell, and Alexander Majors. They were in the transport business, holding government contracts for delivering army supplies to the western frontier. Russell also held a contract for delivering mail to the far west. It was carried by stagecoach, which took weeks to travel the 1,900-mile route between St. Joseph, Missouri, and Sacramento, California. The three men thought that a relay system of fast riders could win them an exclusive government contract to carry the mail. In the winter of 1860, they purchased more than 400 horses and set up 157 relay stations. The stations were placed about 10 miles apart. This was about as far as a horse could travel at a fast pace without endangering the animal. An additional 27 stations were set up as sleeping places for the riders. Mail was carried in a mochila, a Mexican-style pouch that fit over a saddle and was held in place by the rider's weight. Mail weighing up to 20 pounds could fit in a mochila, which was padlocked on both sides for safety.

The riders, who could weigh no more than 125 pounds and were mostly teen boys, would ride 75-100 miles per shift, changing horses frequently along the way. They were expected to ride day or night as required, and at all seasons. On reaching a relay station, they would transfer their *mochila* to a fresh horse and be back in the saddle within seconds. Riders were paid $25 per week, an enormous sum at a time when a dollar a day was considered a fair wage for unskilled labor.

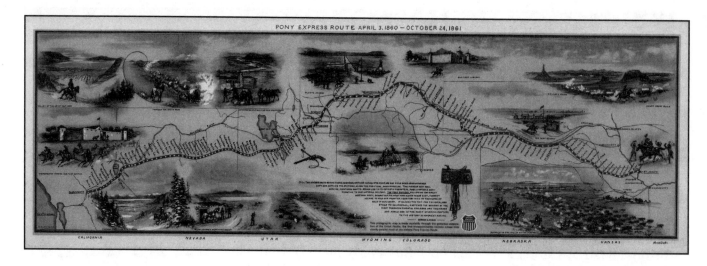
PONY EXPRESS ROUTE APRIL 3, 1860 – OCTOBER 24, 1861

The initial runs east and westbound began on April 3, 1860, and reached their destination ten days later—a pace that skeptics had considered impossible. After this initial success, there were weekly departures in each direction. The Pony Express quickly became an object of popular admiration. Overland stagecoach passengers would be eager to see the riders as they went by, and drivers came to know the schedule in order to accommodate them. Riders were viewed as heroes for the constant danger they faced from rough weather, isolation, and occasional Indian raids. In its 19 months of operation, the Pony Express lost only one shipment, and even that one was found and delivered two years later.

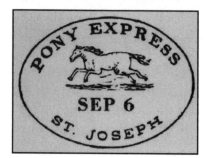

At five dollars per half ounce, the Pony Express was an extravagant way of carrying the mail, when delivery of a standard letter cost a penny. The Express carried business letters and newspapers almost exclusively, but eastern businesses soon discovered that there were few communications so urgent that it was worth the cost. One memorable run in November, 1860, carried news to California of the election to the presidency of Abraham Lincoln. Subsequent deliveries brought the grim news of the break-up of the Union and the start of the Civil War. However, as a business, the Pony Express never turned a profit.

The war, and the urgency of communication, brought a swift end to the Pony Express. A transcontinental telegraph was in operation by late October, 1861. It carried news instantaneously, making the fastest horse seem quaint and obsolete. The Pony Express quickly passed into folklore. Technology had triumphed over romance.

Not completely, however. In today's age of email, text messages, and Twitter, the Pony Express still holds fascination, just as it did in 1930 on the route's 70th anniversary. That year, an 81-year-old gentleman who called himself Bronco Charlie rode horseback from New York City to San Francisco to celebrate the event. He claimed to have been a Pony Express rider during the last five months of its operation, when he would have been all of 11 years old.

27 Joseph Seay distinguishes his point of view about the Pony Express from others' by _____.

   A criticizing it for subjecting poor young boys to danger

   B pointing out that many of the stories told about it are untrue

   C emphasizing that it was a business failure while others emphasize the legend

   D seeing it as an unimportant distraction during a time of great issues in our country

28 Analyze the passage. What are the two main points that Seay makes about the Pony Express, and how does he develop them in his article?

_____

_____

_____

_____

_____

29 Compare and contrast the information and point of view in this article to Mark Twain's account of the Pony Express. How might Joseph Seay have drawn on Twain's primary-source account in writing his article?

_____

_____

_____

_____

_____

30 Write a summary of the article.

_____

_____

_____

_____

_____

GLOSSARY

A

Abecedarians	children learning the alphabet
Adjacent	beside or next to
Antonyms	words with an opposite meaning
Athena	goddess who inspires people with courage
Autobiography	story of a person's life written by that subject

B

Ballad	narrative poem originally written to be sung
Behemoth	large animal; monster
Besieged	surrounded in an attempt to capture
Betrothed	engaged to be married
Biography	story of a person's life written by someone other than the subject
Boon	favor; kindness

C

Caravel	Portuguese ship
Cerebral	appealing to the mind; "brainy"
Characters	the people in a story or play
Chimney-piece	mantelpiece of a fireplace
Claustrophobic	afraid of being in an enclosed space
Climax	the high point of the story
Conflated	formed by a combination of several elements
Conflict	the struggle in a story; can be man versus man, man versus nature, man versus society, or man versus himself
Cossack	cavalry soldier from the Ukraine and southern Russia
Countenance	face
Couplet	two lines that rhyme in a poem

Cytoplasm   the gel-like mass in a cell between the nucleus and the membrane

D

Definitions	words that tell what another word means
Descriptions	words that tell you more about another word
Despot	ruler with unlimited power
Dhow	Egyptian ship
Dialogue	what the characters say in a story or play
Docile	tame; gentle
Dolefully	sorrowfully
Domesticated	tamed
Dramatic License	playing with facts to make more interesting story; not sticking to the facts in a story

E

Endemic	regularly found in an area
Enigmatic	puzzling; mysterious
Epithet	insult
Eradication	wiping out
Exemplary	serving as a warning to others
Exponentially	by several multiples
Exotic	foreign; fascinating because unusual

F

Fable	short story in which characters may be animals portrayed as human types
Fact	statement supported by evidence
Fairy Tale	type of traditional story that involves magical creatures interacting with humans in good and bad ways
Falling Action	the events that follow the climax
Fantasy	story that takes place in an unreal setting or features unreal events; features characters with superhuman powers, magical worlds, or fantastic creatures
Flanks	the right or left side of troop formation
Flashback	events that happened at an earlier time
Folktale	story about ordinary people that contains a lesson about human nature

Foreshadowing		suggestion that some event is to occur in the future
Formidable		tough to deal with
Franchise		a right or privilege
Free verse		poem that does not rhyme or have a rhythm

G

Game	willing to try
Genre	type of literature

H

Habeas corpus	literally "you have a body"—a legal process by which a judge determines whether the government may keep someone in jail
Haiku	Japanese 17-syllable poem usually written in three lines
Hiatus	interruption
Historical Fiction	stories set in a different time period from the past
Homographs	words that are spelled the same but that have different meanings
Hyperbole	exaggerated statement for effect

I

Idioms	phrase that means something other than the literal meaning
Immuring	walling up
Inciting Incident	the event in a story which sets the conflict in motion
Inclement	rainy, snowy, or stormy weather
Infrastructure	physical and organizational structures and services, such as roads and water supply

J

Jim Crow Laws	rules governing what African Americans living in the South were allowed to do

L

League	measurement of distance
Legend	tale from the past about people and events, usually connected to a specific place or time
Limerick	humorous rhyming five-line poem
Lyric Poem	expresses the poet's feelings

(M)

Main Idea	what the story, article, or paragraph is about
Mead	meadow
Metaphor	type of figurative language that compares two unlike things but does not use *like* or *as*
Monologue	a speech delivered in a play to other characters
Montmartre	a famous district in Paris, France
Muse	a goddess who inspires artists
Myth	a story that explains something about nature or a people's customs or beliefs

(N)

Narrative Poem	a poem that tells a story

(O)

Obstinate	stubborn
Onomatopoeia	words that sound like what they are describing
Onus	burden
Opinion	judgment not supported by evidence; what someone thinks or believes
Organelles	small structures within cytoplasm that do specific jobs in a cell

(P)

Paraphernalia	equipment
Perfidy	deliberate falseness; treachery
Personal Essay	a piece of writing in which a person describes and reflects upon something important in that person's life
Personification	giving human characteristics to a concept or inanimate object
Plot	series of events that occur in a story
Point of View	who is telling the story
first-person	the main character is telling the story; uses first person pronouns *I* and *we*
third-person limited omniscient	narrator is limited to knowledge of the thoughts and feelings of only one of the characters; uses third-person pronouns *he, she,* and *they*
third-person omniscient	outside narrator is all-knowing and can reveal the thoughts and feelings of more than one of the characters; uses third-person pronouns *he, she,* and *they*

Poseidon	the sea god, who hates Odysseus
Precipitating	causing an event to abruptly happen
Prediction	what you think the outcome will be
Prefix	part of a word added to beginning of another word that changes the meaning of the word
Preposterous	supremely ridiculous
Profane	vulgar, bad
Purported	claimed

R

Realistic Fiction	story dealing with contemporary issues and setting
Reasoned Judgment	conclusion based on evidence
Refracted	bent from a straight course
Resolution	follows the climax; the explanation of what happens to the characters
Rhyme	repeated sounds at the ends of words
Rhythm	pattern of stressed and unstressed beats in a line of poetry
Rising Action	the events that build to the climax

S

Science Fiction	story that takes place in an unreal setting or features an unreal event; some element of science fact forms the story background
Script	the printed version of a play
Sequence	the order in which actions occur
Setting	the time and place in which a story or play takes place
Shenanigans	mischief or trickery
Silicon	chemical element widely used in electronics
Simile	type of figurative language that compares two unlike things using *as* or *like*
Skirmish	a minor fight during a war
Sonnet	a 14-line poem that follows a formal rhyme scheme
Stage Directions	advice on how actors should move or speak in a play
Stanza	group of lines within a poem, similar to a chapter within a book

Stocks	heavy wooden frame with holes for hands and feet, used as punishment
Straw man	an argument or opinion set up to be easily defeated
Subordinates	people subject to another's orders or supervision
Subservient	acting like an inferior
Suffix	part of a word added to the end of another word that changes the meaning of the word
Summary	short restatement of the ideas in a passage
Symbolism	a symbol that stands for something else
Synonyms	words that have a similar meaning

T

Temperance	19th-century movement against the sale and use of alcoholic drink
Theme	the message or main idea of the story
Tone	the feeling of a story
Truant	staying away from school

W

| **Wantonly** | recklessly; heartlessly |
| **Wrought** | crafted |

NOTES

NOTES